Public Policy and Politics

Series Editors: Colin Fudge ar

Public policy-making in Western democracies is confronted by new pressures. Central values relating to the role of the state, the role of markets and the role of citizenship are now all contested and the consensus built up around the Keynesian welfare state is under challenge. New social movements are entering the political arena: electronic technologies are transforming the nature of employment; changes in demographic structure are creating heightened demands for public services; unforeseen social and health problems are emerging; and, most disturbing, social and economic inequalities are increasing in many countries.

How governments – at international, national and local levels – respond to this developing agenda is the central focus of the *Public Policy and Politics* series. Aimed at a student, professional, practitioner and academic readership, it aims to provide up-to-date, comprehensive and authoritative analyses of public policy-making in practice.

The series is international and interdisciplinary in scope and bridges theory and practice by relating the substance of policy to the politics of the policy-making process.

Public Policy and Politics

Series Editors: Colin Fudge and Robin Hambleton

PUBLISHED

FORTHCOMING

Councillors in Crisis

The Public and Private Worlds of Local Councillors

Jacqueline Barron
Gerald Crawley
Tony Wood

MACMILLAN

© Jacqueline Barron, Gerald Crawley and Tony Wood 1991

All rights reserved. No reproduction, copy or transmission
of this publication may be made without written permission.

No paragraph of this publication may be reproduced, copied or
transmitted save with written permission or in accordance with
the provisions of the Copyright, Designs and Patents Act 1988,
or under the terms of any licence permitting limited copying
issued by the Copyright Licensing Agency, 33–4 Alfred Place,
London WC1E 7DP.

Any person who does any unauthorised act in relation to
this publication may be liable to criminal prosecution and
civil claims for damages.

First published 1991

Published by
MACMILLAN EDUCATION LTD
Houndmills, Basingstoke, Hampshire RG21 2XS
and London
Companies and representatives
throughout the world

Edited and typeset by Povey/Edmondson
Okehampton and Rochdale, England

Printed in Hong Kong

British Library Cataloguing in Publication Data
Barron, Jacqueline 1943–
Councillors in crisis: the public and private worlds of
local councillors. — (Public policy and politics).
1. England. Local authorities. Councillors
I. Title II. Crawley, Gerald 1938– III. Wood, Tony 1938–
IV. Series
352.005
ISBN 0-333-49034-7 (hardcover)
ISBN 0-333-49035-5 (paperback)

Series Standing Order   (Public Policy and Politics)

If you would like to receive future titles in this series as they are
published, you can make use of our standing order facility. To place a
standing order please contact your bookseller or, in case of difficulty,
write to us at the address below with your name and address and the
name of the series. Please state with which title you wish to begin your
standing order. (If you live outside the UK we may not have the rights
for your area, in which case we will forward your order to the publisher
concerned.)

Customer Services Department, Macmillan Distribution Ltd,
Houndmills, Basingstoke, Hampshire, RG21 2XS, England

Contents

List of Tables and Figures

Tables

Figures

vi

Acknowledgements

We wish to thank a number of people for their support in making this book possible.

We are indebted to the Trustees of the Leverhulme Trust who were willing to fund our original research project which explored the relationship between the private and public worlds of local politicians. We also wish to thank the Bristol Polytechnic Research Committee who funded us for two years on a related investigation dealing with the recruitment of local councillors.

Neither of these research investigations would have been successful, however, without the wholehearted cooperation of councillors, candidates, other political activists and their respective spouses. They invited us, total strangers, to their homes and spoke to us, at great length, at a time which was often particularly busy for them, about matters of a highly confidential nature. We are grateful for the confidence they showed in us and we hope we have kept their trust.

In carrying out the research and in writing up our findings, our debts are numerous. The staff of the Computer Centre at Bristol Polytechnic, notably David Gethin, were particularly helpful in introducing us to the use of information technology and gave us their unfailing support.

We are grateful to the secretaries of the Department of Economics and Social Science – Ena Briers and Christine Hunt – who provided invaluable support to the research team.

We particularly wish to acknowledge our indebtedness to John Hilbourne, who, prior to taking up an appointment with the Department of Education and Science, was a member of the research team. He was involved at the formative stage and participated fully in the making of key decisions associated with our first research project. Also, we are grateful for the helpful comment and guidance of Steven Kennedy and Robin Hambleton.

Finally, we would like to acknowledge the support of our colleagues in the Department of Economics and Social Sciences who have given critical reaction to ideas, been tolerant of our preoccupation and have refrained from complaining when the exigencies of the research prevented our fulfilling other commitments.

JACQUELINE BARRON
GERALD CRAWLEY
TONY WOOD

Guide to Reading the Book

Why have local government? What contribution does it make to the good government of the country? What contribution should it make in this regard? What is the value of local elections? These are some of the questions which are increasingly asked today and which are the outcome of the challenges that local authorities have faced for more than a decade.

If these questions are to be answered with conviction and authority, the informed public need to know more about the person who should be the focus of these discussions – the democratically elected councillor. We hope that this book makes a valuable contribution to the debate about the place of local democracy in the British political system of the 1990s.

We have divided the central part of the book into two sections: THE PUBLIC WORLD and THE PRIVATE WORLD. We, however, see this conventional distinction between the 'public' and the 'private' merely as a starting point and as a way of structuring the book. We hope that readers will come to share the views of many of the people to whom we spoke that the 'public' and the 'private' worlds of local politicians, both men and women, are closely interrelated.

Why do a small minority of people in Britain today take part in local political activity? In Chapter 2 we summarise the main reasons people gave us for entering local politics – primarily a wish to serve the community or to serve the party – and outline the ways in which they were recruited. Others explained why they were not prepared to stand for the council and their remarks throw light upon the unrepresentative nature of council membership and in particular the low proportion of women members. We suggest, in conclusion, that councillors are carried into office on a tide of party persuasion often in the absence of alternative prospective candidates.

And how do those councillors who get elected manage their workloads? This is the starting point of Chapter 3. We argue that earlier official studies of the work done by councillors grossly understated the work that members did. By meticulously collecting detailed information from councillors, we established that workloads are nearly twice that of official estimates.

How is the family affected and what kind of support does the local politician receive from the partner? These are two of the questions which we consider in Chapter 4. We have found that the nature of that support depends upon whether the partner is a husband or wife and whether the politician is a member of a 'political household'. The ways in which political activity can enrich the lives of politicians (and their partners) is the subject of Chapter 5. We also examine the ways in which politicians draw boundaries (or choose not to draw them) between their public and private lives. In both these chapters, we also consider briefly the reported consequences of political activity for the children of the household.

The financial and employment costs of political activity are the subjects of Chapter 6. As politics can take up a large part of an individual's life, it is difficult to combine this with a paid job. Councillors receive attendance allowances, but these do not compensate, for example, for the loss of promotion. Some people are content to see their activity as a 'career-substitute' but others have to juggle their paid work and their public responsibilities in ways which please neither their employers nor their political colleagues.

In the last part of the book we draw together a variety of themes. Chapter 7 spells out a typology of roles that councillors play: those for whom politics is a part-time hobby; those who see it as an all-consuming vocation; and those who regard political work as a full-time job which should be paid. Chapter 8 puts forward recommendations and looks at how some other countries are trying to resolve similar problems. We compare the different situations of local and national politicians and argue that councils could do much to support the diversity of roles which councillors play. We comment on how far recent legislation is likely to widen the pool of potential council recruits.

Note: We make considerable use of verbatim quotations, and have given each of our informants a pseudonym.

PART I
INTRODUCTION

1 Introduction

One hundred years ago, in 1889, the first elections were held for county councils. Since that time the principle of representative local democracy has been widely accepted as a fundamental feature of the British political system. Yet, today, local government is in crisis. From Westminster and Whitehall it faces criticism and disdain. From within, it faces doubt and disunity.

This book is concerned with the individual at the centre of this crisis – the councillor. It looks at how the councillor is recruited and at the work that the councillor does. It does not, however, look merely at the public aspects of the councillor's world. It also draws upon extensive and confidential interviews with elected members and their partners and examines the private world – the effects on husbands and wives and children and the implications for employment and social life. In these ways it represents a radical departure from conventional political science literature. It is a book about the private face of politics.

Expansion and consensus

For thirty years after the Second World War local government increased in economic and political significance. The loss of certain functions – for example, hospitals and electricity generation – was more than compensated for by the growth and diversification of those services, such as education, which remained the responsibility of local councils. By 1976 the share of the gross domestic product going to local government had increased by almost 70 per cent and there seemed no reason to doubt that the future offered further growth. In 1969 the Royal Commission on Local Government in England talked optimistically about the 'general tendency . . . towards the expansion of existing local government services' and 'the steady rise in local government's share of public sector expenditure . . .' (Royal Commission on Local Government in England 1969 Vol. I, p. 56).

The Conservative Government of the early 1970s appeared to accept the enhanced economic and political significance of local government. In 1971 it restated its support for local democracy:

> The Government are . . . determined to return power to those people who should exercise decisions locally, and to ensure that local government is given every opportunity to take that initiative effectively, speedily and with vigour. (Department of Environment 1971b, p. 6)

At the same time the Government spoke of the need 'to preserve and strengthen the financial responsibility of local government and to minimize detailed intervention by central departments' (Department of Environment 1971a, p. 1). A year later, with reorganisation imminent, it enthusiastically endorsed corporate management within local authorities and urged councillors to embrace the expansive sentiments of the Bains Report which argued that local government should have '. . . within its purview the overall economic, cultural and physical well-being of [the] community . . .' (Bains 1972, p. 6).

In these statements the Heath administration endorsed the broad consensus between party leaders and academics concerning the general benefits of local government. This consensus, while never clearly expressed, saw the system of local government as offering a number of advantages. The local authority, being independently accountable to local voters, was an alternative focus of political allegiance and a check on the centralised power of the state. Additionally, it offered voters a form of local participation which was readily accessible and which called for only a limited commitment. Once elected to office, only councillors, in Mill's terms, had the 'competence in details' – the local knowledge and the ability to adapt national policies efficiently to local circumstances.

This postwar consensus concerning the intrinsic value of local government no longer exists. For ten years or more, local authorities have been the target of a very large volume of legislation which seeks to define, delegate, limit, 'cap', prescribe, contract-out, privatise and hive-off the activities of local councils. As one commentator has observed:

Supporters of local government can make a strong case that it has been cash controlled, constrained, supervised, bypassed and generally downtrodden during the Thatcher years. (Mather 1989)

Local authorities have reacted to this legislation in very different ways. A minority – some of those controlled by Conservative groups or by independent councillors – have tried breathlessly to keep pace with it or even one step ahead. Council houses have been sold off to housing associations. Schools have been given their own budgets to manage. Sports centres have been formed into companies and then been subject to management 'buy-outs'.

Most local authorities, however, have reacted in a more cautious and defensive manner. Capital expenditure has been drastically curtailed for fear of generating additional future demands on local revenue. Current expenditure has been concealed by subtle techniques of creative accounting. Expansion of existing services has slowed (if not stopped) and vacancies amongst staffs have gone unfilled. As a precaution, individual council departments have been reorganised in anticipation of the need to submit 'in-house' bids for services subject to competitive tender. The requirements of national legislation have generally been met but often with little energy and less enthusiasm.

The effect of these many contested changes has been to thrust local authorities and their members to the centre stage of national and local political debate. 'Municipal socialists' are arrayed against those who foresee the local authority of the 1990s as being little more than a holding company which meets periodically to award contracts to the private sector. At stake are the issues which have, in earlier times, been the subject of merely academic debate: What is the value of local government? What is the difference between local government and local administration? What is the relevance of party politics to local affairs? What should be the appropriate role for the elected member? (See Stewart and Stoker 1989.)

The values implicit in the earlier consensus about local government – liberty, participation and efficiency – were correspondingly reflected in three ways in which members could choose to define their roles. Those who championed the interests of their constituents were the caseworkers. Those who sought to define the local public interest by participating in decision-making were the policymakers. Those who were concerned with the effective and efficient implementation of national legislation were the managers. Today, in contrast, members' roles are unclear, their abilities are questioned and their future existence is debated.

The caseworker in crisis

As caseworker, the councillor has always been a focus of complaints and protests even in the era of local government expansion and adequate resources. Since the 1970s, however, this particular aspect of the councillor's public duties has become more onerous. The reduction in the number of councillors following the reorganisation of local government in 1974 has approximately doubled the average number of constituents whom councillors are required to serve and in rural areas, also, wards or electoral divisions are disproportionately larger.

Councillors as caseworkers face a knowledgeable and vociferous electorate. A recent survey concluded that there was generally a high level of awareness of local government services and that those who had stayed on at school beyond the present school-leaving age (an increasing proportion) were more knowledgeable than those who had left earlier (Widdicombe 1986d, Table 2.2 and p. 99). Today, when cuts to services are under discussion in most authorities, there is likely to be heightened pressure on the ward member not only from local electors but also from pressure groups like amenity and tenants' associations. When such groups cultivate media interest the member must be seen to be playing a prominent protective role.

What value do people place on their councillor as caseworker? We know that the level of complaints directed at local authorities suggests that voters do attach some value to the ready accessibility of local councils. Survey evidence shows that more than a quarter of all voters had complained at some time or another and the more knowledgeable the voter the more likely he or she is to want to complain (Widdicombe 1986d, Tables 4.1, 4.3). While councillors are not the main recipients of complaints (officers receive twice as many) they, together with Members of Parliament, are seen as the most important and effective focus of protest against 'really wrong' decisions (Widdicombe 1986d, Table 4.7. See also MORI 1986, p. 5).

This public confidence in the capacity of the councillor to secure redress on behalf of local people has to be weighed carefully in the light of other evidence. Much of this suggests that members are not always reliable champions of their constituents' interests. In contrast to most MPs, for example, councillors, particularly those in the majority group, are part of the process of debate and decision which may have given rise to the constituent's complaint in the first instance. Where these decisions are taken in the context of intense party conflict, the member who has received the complaint may be very reluctant to pursue it with vigour to the point of politically embarrassing party colleagues (Lewis *et al.* 1987, p. 5). Political partisanship may also influence the councillor's reaction in another way. Approximately one-third of the complaints investigated by the Commissioner for Local Administration in 1987 were referred by the complainants themselves and in nearly half of these councillors had refused to assist the constituent (Commission for Local Administration 1987).

A high level of partisanship may also help to explain an apparent paradox. Surveys have reported a high (and rising) level of public satisfaction with local councils and considerable support for elected local government (Widdicombe 1986d, pp. 99–100, MORI 1986, p. iii, Consumers' Association 1989, Miller 1988, Ch. 3). Yet there is a disturbing residue of dissatisfaction. Recent research has found that as many as 42 per cent of respondents had wanted to complain but only 26 per cent had actually complained. Interestingly, those people who were most opposed to party politics in local government were more dissatisfied but were less likely to make a formal complaint than those who felt the party system was preferable. Almost one-third of those who had not actually complained seemed convinced that 'they would not listen' or 'nothing would get done' (Widdicombe 1986d, pp. 50–53).

Lewis and his associates come to a similar conclusion and stress the extent to which the council itself can inhibit or encourage complainants (Lewis *et al.* 1987). They report that less than half of local authorities claim to have an authority-wide procedure for handling complaints. Of these only a small proportion publicise their com-plaints machinery and many authorities with seemingly excellent procedures have filed them away and allowed them to fall into disuse. They conclude 'that there exists a submerged body of complaints which administrative cultures help to suppress' (ibid., p. 221).

In a similar manner, individual councillors can inhibit or encourage complaints as part of their own distinctive definition of their public duties. As we show in a later chapter the significance of casework in the total load on members varies very considerably and we would strongly endorse the comment that members can have a powerful influence when they do decide to take up the cudgels on their constituent's behalf (ibid., p. 5).

The policymaker in crisis

The councillor as policymaker is the most powerful justification of democratically elected local authorities. More than 20 years ago, an influential official report spelt out the duties of councillors as policymakers:

> It is the members who should take and be responsible for the key decisions on objectives, and on the means and plans to attain them. It is they who must periodically review the position as part of their function of directing and controlling. (Maud 1967a, p. 38)

It went on to consider the complementary activities of officers:

> It is the officers who should provide the necessary staff work and advice which will enable the members to identify the problems, set the objectives and select the means and plans to attain them. It is the officers who should direct and co-ordinate the necessary action, and see that material is presented to enable members to review progress and check performance. (Maud 1967a, p. 38)

How far were such statements an accurate description of the practices of local councils? To what extent were policy decisions actually taken by councillors? Were officers really subordinate to members in this regard? Answers to these questions are best understood in the light of the ideological agreement about the proper role of local authorities between the Conservative and Labour parties which existed until the 1970s and which acted as the political ballast for the expansion of local government which we referred to earlier. Two assumptions were central to this agreement. There was, firstly, the 'welfare consensus' between the parties which saw elected local government as 'a prime vehicle in the drive to create the Welfare State' (Stoker 1988, p. 7). Throughout the 1950s and 1960s, local government both increased its range of responsibilities and improved standards of existing provision. Secondly, there was a pervading sense of success and certainty. Services had grown in response to need. There was a 'right' solution to most of the problems perceived in our towns and countryside – pursued by central government and by local authorities (Stewart and Stoker 1989, p. 244).

To the official mind, at this time, organised party groups on councils scarcely existed and certainly warranted no special study or investigation (Maud 1967a, p. 112). In most local councils, for the greater part of the period up to the 1970s, policy decisions were taken in an apolitical context with occasional disagreement over how best to achieve greater efficiency and modernisation. Many councils were dominated by independent councillors and even where a party held a majority of the seats, control by the party group of the process of making policy was largely nominal. To many academic observers party competition seemed largely irrelevant. Policy was the preserve of committee chairmen (*sic*) and chief officers (Bulpitt 1983, Rhodes 1985, Stoker 1988).

Today, for many councillors, the context within which they make policy is one of heightened ideological conflict and personal rancour. A recent inquiry has commented:

> there can be no doubt that local government is increasingly seen today as an arena in which to pursue ideological values and objectives and to seek to bring about radical change. Broad policy statements are thus transferred from manifestos to become the overall policy of the authority – in the case of one Conservative London borough, 'to reduce the size of the public sector', and for a Labour district council, 'to bring about a fundamental shift of power and resources in favour of working class people'. (Widdicombe 1986b, p. 59)

The same inquiry talked of the increasingly acrimonious nature of debate in council and the breakdown of the traditional patterns of social interaction between the parties (Widdicombe 1986b, p. 35).

There are now two different worlds of local political ideology represented, by the Conservative Right and the Labour Left. For the Conservative Right,

> Inside every fat and bloated local authority there is a slim one struggling to get out. (Ridley, N. 1988, p. 26).

For the Labour Left, local government

> didn't seem to be much more than old white men talking about rubbish collection . . . the way forward is to commit people from the bottom up – in a jigsaw . . . that doesn't ignore national and international parameters, but relates to them. (Boddy and Fudge 1984, pp. 244 and 263)

Heightened political conflict is not restricted to relations between competing party groups. Increasingly acrimonious relations within groups have been reported. While political labels can mislead as much as inform, to be 'wet' or 'dry' (for a Conservative) or 'soft-left' or 'hard-left' (for a Labour member) is seen by many councillors to be of critical importance when policy decisions are to be taken. Such divisions within groups appear to be related to the decline of the traditional authoritarian style of group leadership in favour of a more consultative mode of operation (Widdicombe 1986b, p. 90, pp. 199–200).

Many consequences have flowed from the increased political polarisation of councils in the last 10 years. Members of Labour-controlled authorities have been called upon to make policy on issues such as nuclear energy and women's rights which have rarely, if ever, appeared on council agendas in previous decades. Conservative councillors, arguing a more 'minimalist' view of local government, have angrily disputed the relevance of these questions, but when out-voted all share in the extra commitment of time and effort that these questions demand.

Traditional relations between members and officers have also been challenged. In less polarised times, senior officers determined a committee's agenda. Today, matters are much less clear-cut. The content of agendas has become more a subject of 'negotiation' between chief officers, the incumbent of the committee's chair and, possibly, the majority group on the committee. This has lead to a more fundamental question. The Widdicombe Committee reported:

> the role of the professional chief officer is being questioned by councillors who wish to intervene more in day-to-day management, often seeing the style of implementation of a policy as part of the policy itself rather than a separate process . . . (Widdicombe 1986a, p. 104)

In essence, the distinction so widely drawn in the past between the making of policy and the implementation of that policy is no longer accepted and is itself, for some councillors, a 'policy issue' of the very greatest significance. The councillor who takes a policy decision is inevitably asserting a particular (and possibly partisan) definition of the public interest. In earlier, more consensual days, the 'public interest' had the character of the matter-of-fact, something more assumed than demonstrated, something that was unquestioningly the outcome of the council's weighty deliberations.

If we are to understand the contrast with the present, the absence of ideological consensus between the parties provides only part of the explanation. It omits the growth in diversity and complexity of local interest groups and the wider social changes of which these groups are the manifestation. A number of observers have identified the many social changes to which local politicians are now required to respond (Widdicombe 1986e, Ch. 4, Young, K. 1985 in Jowell, R. and Witherspoon, S. 1985, Stoker 1988b). These are occurring in all aspects of social life as, for example, patterns of employment, gender relations and family life become more varied. Communities and groups within the ward, the city, or the county are more diversified. As one recent commentator has described it:

> the world of local interest groups is closer now to a conscript army in its diversity, range of opinion, its disgruntled participation and propensity to rebellion! (Stoker 1988b, p. 124)

These groups are much more inclined to challenge the definition of the public interest proclaimed by members. They are more able than earlier generations to offer and articulate their own conception of the public good. They will, alternatively, dispute the existence of anything other than sectional, class, racial or gender interests. There is, it is argued, no wider general good for the councillor as policymaker to serve. The 'public' interest is dead.

The manager in crisis

There was never a golden age of local government when local councillors were free to do as they wished. The independence of local authorities has always been limited by acts of Parliament, statutory instruments and circulars – the main 'products' of British non-executant central government. By these means, Whitehall and Westminster have sought to define, regulate and guide local authorities as the main mechanism for the delivery of a wide range of public services.

This measure of 'control' has, however, traditionally been both distant and often imprecise. The non-executant character of central government meant that it rarely involved itself directly in building housing estates, schools, shopping centres and roads. As a consequence, it accumulated only a limited knowledge and understanding of how policies were implemented at street, ward and city level. Even as recently as 1977 an official investigation candidly concluded:

> Central government's knowledge about what is happening at the local level can best be described as patchy. This is true both in general and in relation to specific attempts by central government to influence the provision of services. (Central Policy Review Staff, 1977, p. 33)

This incapacity of central government has been one aspect of the 'dual polity' wherein the centre has sought to distance itself from 'Low Politics' (of council houses and schools) in order to enhance its autonomy in 'High Politics' (of defence and foreign policy) (Bulpitt 1983, Rhodes 1985). In effect, councillors were left with extensive discretion to exercise in the management of their very imprecisely defined statutory duties. The centre

> was insulated from [the] localities which were allowed considerable operational autonomy. (Rhodes 1985)

Primary education had to be provided, but should it start at the age of three or five? Should secondary education be selective in character? What kind of regime should operate in children's homes? What level of rents should be charged council house tenants? Most important, how much money should be raised from the rates and which services were to be given the highest priority? In these and other matters, councillors were largely allowed to make their own judgements. The centre paid them the compliment that they knew best.

The intense and comprehensive legislative activity of the centre in the 1980s suggests that the distinction between 'High Politics' and 'Low Politics' is no longer valid. Clearly, the Thatcher government holds a very different view of elected members from that held by previous governments. Elected members cannot be relied upon to judge wisely between the local and the national interest. They cannot be relied upon to arbitrate between competing and conflicting groups at the local level. The message from the government is that councillors' own definitions of the local interest, whether Conservative, Liberal Democrat or Labour, are necessarily flawed and have to be set aside. As Jones and Stewart have commented:

> The implication is that local authorities and councillors are more unpopular than any other part of government; that they are less trusted, more corrupt and more inefficient. (Jones and Stewart 1983, p. 14).

This systematic contempt for and disregard of the views of elected members is clearly shown in successive acts of Parliament dealing with council finances. These have tried to coerce councillors (with only modest success!) to accept the centre's view of what particular councils should spend. In place of councillors' judgements have been the judgements of – not ministers – but Whitehall officials – albeit in the name of the Secretary of State. Each year different (and often conflicting) varieties of expenditure 'targets' have been given to local councils. Frequently, one year's 'target' has borne little relationship to the following year's. Councils in closely similar circumstances have been given very different expenditure 'targets'. Minister after minister promised vainly that the calculation of central government grant to councils would be 'fairer', 'simpler', less erratic (Travers 1986, p. 83; Department of the Environment 1986, paras 4.16–4.18).

In due course, two major audit bodies (not noted for the unrestrained use of language) employed such terms as 'worthless', 'inconsistent', 'discriminatory', 'ambiguous' about the centre's attempt to substitute its own detailed judgements about spending for those of councillors (Audit Commission 1984, National Audit Office 1985).

In major service areas, the collective discretion of elected members has been set aside. In the field of planning and economic regeneration, for example, eleven urban development corporations have been established in various cities in England and Wales. These have been given more extensive development control powers than local councils normally possess. They have been vested with land (often previously improved by the councils themselves) and 'given access to large amounts of public money' (House of Commons Employment Committee 1988, para. 96). It is hardly surprising that many councillors in these areas felt that given the same powers and resources they could achieve results at least as good as the development corporations and with much less risk of disregarding local community opinion and interests.

In a related area, housing, the effectiveness of local authorities as landlords has been questioned. The 'New Right' has depicted housing authorities as incompetent bureaucracies pursuing their own selfish ends with taxpayers' money, insensitive to the wishes of their tenants (Breton and Wintrobe 1982, Niskanen 1973). A major report has concluded, however, that these views 'have little basis in reality' and that there is neither a resource nor an organisational crisis in local authority housing (Maclennan Report 1989, p. 124).

Councillors of all parties have stressed the need for low-cost rented accommodation for local people (Association of District Councils 1989). Homelessness, according to the Audit Commission, has been increasing over a long period of time, across all types of authority, in different regions, under all types of political control and with widely varying housing policies. (Audit Commission 1989, p. 10)

In spite of the accumulation by councils of considerable funds from the earlier sale of council houses, central government has severely curtailed new house building by councils. In future these housing needs are to be met by housing associations working through the Housing Corporation. All new tenancies will be subject to a system of 'affordable' market rents. Apart from causing considerable problems for tenants and potential tenants, this legislation will leave the council with statutory responsibility for the homeless – but without satisfactory means of relieving it. Councillors, in the meantime, will be faced with an increasing number of complaints and demands from disgruntled citizens whose housing needs are unlikely ever to be met.

In education, also, the collective experience and judgements of councillors has been devalued. This is in spite of considerable evidence of satisfaction amongst regular users of schools and colleges (Jones and Stewart 1983, p. 14; Audit Commission 1986, pp. 11–14; *The Times Educational Supplement* 29 January 1988). The Education Reform Act 1988, in establishing a 'National Curriculum', has removed what little influence elected members had over what happens in the classroom. Furthermore, councillors' powers to adapt educational provision to meet changing local demands and circumstances appear to have been greatly curtailed. Even before the Act of 1988, councillors had been criticised by the Audit Commission and the Department of Education and Science for not using their powers to the full. More schools should have been closed. More empty school places should have been taken out of use. Following the Act which granted to school governing bodies the power to seek total independence of the local education authority – to 'opt out' – it is difficult to see how councillors can shape and adapt local education systems to meet changing circumstances in an intelligent and responsive manner.

What is left for those councillors with an interest in education? Will overseeing the residual advisory services, tinkering with the formula which distributes money to 'locally managed' schools and debating broad 'strategy' provide a sufficiently attractive and challenging agenda either for existing members or for those few members of the public who are prepared to consider being councillors?

Perspectives on local government in crisis

All these separate changes (and many others) have appeared to some MPs, voters and councillors to be fully justified. For them, individual legislative proposals had considerable merits and had, in their view, been endorsed by voters in successive general elections. But the cumulative significance of all the measures has been obscured. The brisk and confident step-by-step approach of successive Secretaries of State, aided by extensive use of the guillotine to curtail debate in the House of Commons, has provided Parliament with scarcely any opportunity to take stock and to examine the wider effects upon the body politic of local government.

One measure of the effect is in the volume of legislation which has been pushed through Parliament and which has required the deliberations of councillors. From 1979 to mid-1990 Parliament passed 124 Acts applying directly to local government – of which 14 dealt with local government finance (House of Commons 1990). One major professional body has commented:

> the government unleashed a barrage of legislation onto local government . . . (CIPFA 1989, *Local Government Trends*, 1988, p. 5)

This 'barrage' has had a perverse and surprising effect: the demand on councillors' time and energies has, in the view of many, increased substantially. This is something which we will explore in some detail in a later chapter.

Another consequence has been to compel members and officers, the press and academics to analyse and speculate upon the intentions and actions of the government. Two broad views have emerged. The first view emphasises the fragmented, impulsive and inconsistent nature of the government's approach. Critics point, for example, to the unexpected announcement at the start of the 1983 general election campaign that the abolition of the Greater

London Council and the metropolitan county councils was to be included in the Conservative Party manifesto. It was suggested that the idea was made up in considerable haste as a manifesto 'fill-up' with little consideration of its consequences (Chandler 1988, p. 162; Leach 1989, p. 102). As Stoker has written:

> The inclusion of these proposals . . . bears the hallmarks of a last minute insertion, at the behest of the Prime Minister herself, based to a degree on her antipathy towards the policies and propaganda of the GLC and her personal dislike of its leader, Ken Livingstone. (Stoker 1988, p. 140).

A similar view is that of local authority finance officers who see a lack of strategy as the cause of concern. In a review of the 'barrage of legislation' they concluded that the government's actions had no guiding policy. Local government legislation had been approached in a very piecemeal fashion spurred on by political stimuli rather than reasoned research and consultation. The government stated that rates were to be abolished but no research was carried out on the likely impact of the community charge and the feasibility of charge-capping. Similarly, with respect to competitive tendering, the injection of market forces may increase efficiency but no thought had been given to effectiveness (CIPFA 1989, p. 5). The government, however, sees its relationship with local authorities as pragmatic and undoctrinaire. As Nicholas Ridley has argued:

> Government's role at the centre is that of consultant prescribing remedies. (Ridley 1988, p. 26)

If the government was in the highly competitive 'consultancy' marketplace would it find any local authority clients?

The second view contradicts the first. It infers that the government does indeed have a strategy, has made a critical political judgement and has evolved a programme which, for reasons of political convenience, it chooses not to declare at the moment. In these ways, say the critics, the government is influenced by the ideologues of the 'New Right' who see local authorities as bureaucracies beyond the control of their elected members, subject to weak electoral constraints and responsive only to the clamours

of employees and the shouts of lobbyists. Pirie cogently expresses
this view of public sector bureaucracies:

> The monopoly position [of public bureaucracies] combined with
> the unlikelihood of the public sector employee losing his (*sic*) job
> through lack of custom, have created conditions under which the
> desires of the consumer are of little account. The interests of
> those engaged in the production of the service loom much larger
> in consideration when service quality is determined. Much is
> done for the convenience of the administration and the work-
> force which would never be accepted in any private service. (Pirie
> 1982)

This perspective emphasises that the Government's programme is
more than a mixture of *ad hoc* measures, electoral ambition, power
politics and belief in the enterprise spirit. There is an ideological
coherence which holds together the various initiatives and pieces of
legislation (Stoker 1988, p. 253; Leach 1989, p. 119; Travers 1989).

Whether or not the Government has a 'strategy' for local
government, there is a wide measure of agreement that relations
between local councils and the centre have undergone significant
change. Different observers bring their own interpretations to this
general theme.

Some writers stress that informal consultation arrangements
have broken down in many areas and the traditional methods of
creating a consensus before embarking on major legislative change
have been abandoned. Local–central conflicts have become ende-
mic. Local councils have increasingly sought to determine their
rights and duties through the legal system and the courts and – in
the case of community charge-capping – through appeal to the
House of Lords (Loughlin 1985, pp. 65–6).

Others stress the dangerous concentration of power at the centre.
There has been a movement of key decisions from the local level to
national level – far from those on whom they have an impact.
There has been a strengthening of the central bureaucracy, a
decrease in the visibility and accessibility of government. Responsiveness to local needs has been replaced by an increase in
uniformity (Jones and Stewart 1983, pp. 10–11).

Many observers argue that this centralisation of statutory and
bureaucratic power has not been accompanied by a centralisation

of competence and effectiveness. Travers, writing about the numerous and partly abortive attempts to control local spending, comments:

> [I]f we look simply at the record of what has happened, it is hard to see just what the Government has achieved, in their own terms, despite the vast amount of attention they have given to local spending. (Travers, T. 1986a)

Stoker, also, argues that in spite of aggressive attacks by the Government, reductions in expenditure have been only modest and in no sense has local government been pushed into a minimalist role (Stoker 1989, pp. 152–3). Jones and Stewart go further; they believe that an increase in central government power may actually reduce the ability of the political system to resolve the problems it faces.

> To centralise in government may appear to strengthen its power, but it may well weaken the ability to use that power effectively. (Jones and Stewart 1983, p. 4)

In a similar vein, for Dunleavy and Rhodes central intervention has clearly increased. But the picture is less clear for 'central control'. The record of the 1980s appears to be one of declining public effectiveness – both central and local – which the Government has belatedly recognised. As a result ministers are now putting their trust in

> . . . new forms of micro-local organisations to erode local authorities' 'monopoly control' over schooling and public housing from below. (Dunleavy and Rhodes 1988, p. 143).

When this occurs what will be left for councillors as managers to manage?

Recent legislation: confusion and inconsistency

The fragmented and inconsistent approach of the government is illustrated by recent legislation. Some decisions appear to be an expression of a new-found confidence in local government. Local authorities will soon have extended responsibilities for community care, the protection of the environment and economic development. Moreover, since April 1990, councils' spending has ceased to be part of the Treasury's system of financial control. Travers has commented that this latter change

> goes further towards local autonomy than anything considered in years . . . the implications are considerable, particularly the symbolic implication about the nature of central government control over local government activity. (Travers 1988)

In effect, the government has accepted what a number of independent local government observers have been saying for a number of years. Neither federal states like the US or Canada, nor unitary states like France or the Netherlands seek to control local government revenue expenditure.

Against these welcome developments must be set a tidal wave of legislation the effect of which enhances the formal power of the centre at the expense of local authorities. The 1988 Local Government Finance Act has brought radical and much discussed change to the financial regime under which local councils operate. The introduction of the community charge, the nationalisation of the business rate and a new (and cruder) way of calculating grant support for councils has produced the 'gearing effect' whereby a council's 'overspend' of 1 per cent is magnified into a 4 per cent increase in the bill presented to chargepayers.

The prolonged legal battle over 'charge-capping' in the spring and summer of 1990 encapsulated the Janus-like character of the government's approach to local authorities. In one breath, the community charge was presented as the prime instrument to bring about effective accountability to local voters. In the next, many local authorities were described as profligate with public money and some were made subject to statutory capping of their charges even where voters had endorsed councils' spending plans. Other provisions of the same legislation introduced new controls on capital finance, extended compulsory competitive tendering and further reduced the housing activities of local authorities.

Only one year later, a further set of far-reaching measures began to affect councils. The Local Government and Housing Act 1989 continued the trend of giving to the Secretary of State the discretion to make regulations which defined the detailed provisions of the legislation. As a result, the large amount of this 'secondary legislation' that has emerged has not been subject to full Parliamentary scrutiny and debate and, in many instances, has been beyond the capacity of the civil servants at the Department of the Environment to execute in the limited time available.

In this way, measures have been passed which prescribe the political composition of council committees, impose a formal legal framework on relationships between elected members and certain senior officers, introduce restrictions on the political activities of some local government officers and institute, in the face of considerable hostility from the local authority associations, a restricted pattern of allowances for elected members. The significance of these measures for councillors will be discussed in the final chapter.

The distinctiveness of our approach

Since the 1960s the world of the local politician has attracted much attention. It has been the focus of considerable academic activity and the subject of at least three major official investigations. (Maud Report 1967, Robinson Report 1977, Widdicombe Report 1986). Most of these studies have concentrated on the 'public' world of the politician. This is seen as something separate from the 'private' world of family, employment and leisure. Occasionally this 'private' world has been granted a passing acknowledgement. For example, Collins, in discussing the social background and motivation of councillors, says that

> The availability of new members [i.e. councillors] depends to a large extent on their ability to arrange their affairs to facilitate the necessarily heavy demands upon a councillor's time. This tends to limit new members to those for whom the financial sacrifice is not too great, whose jobs allow the necessary flexibility of hours and whose family and social commitments permit lengthy absence from home during leisure hours. (Collins 1978a)

Similarly, Fudge, Murie and Ring (1979) in their innovative report looked briefly at the private world of newly elected councillors. Their study suggested new lines of inquiry but most of their comments were speculative. Moreover, the characteristics of the sample (which consisted solely of very recent recruits, only three of whom were women, and only one a Labour member) necessarily limits the relevance which can be placed on their conclusions.

For most political scientists, however, this private world is not a proper field of study. As a result, we know little about the effects of political activism or council membership on individuals and their partners and families. Conversely, we cannot judge how far and in what ways decisions in the 'public' world – whether or not to stand for election or which party meeting to attend – are affected by such factors as family composition, marital status and employment.

A further result of this conventional focus is that the gender of politicians has received only limited attention. While there has been some concern about the under-representation of women in local government (Bristow 1980, Evans 1984, Hills 1980 and 1981, Martlew *et al.* 1985 and Martlew 1988) there has been no attempt to look at the ways in which gender influences how the politician's role is interpreted, or whether the impact of political activity on private life is different for men and women. Sociological studies of gender roles and of 'dual-career' families indicate that full-time employment may conflict with social expectations regarding women's role in the home. This suggested to us that women entering local politics experience extra difficulties in combining their public and private commitments.

The absence of significant studies of this kind meant that there were few data upon which we could draw. Furthermore, as we were interested in private and domestic matters, the material would be of a sensitive nature. We decided, therefore, to interview councillors and other local politicians (and their spouses or other partners) in such a way as to allow them to talk about their situation as candidly and at whatever length they chose with as little intrusion from us as possible. By means of these 'semi-structured' interviews we hoped to gather 'qualitatively' interesting comments rather than the kind of quantifiable factual information which is the product of the sample survey or opinion polling approach. In total we carried out more than 300 interviews involving 107 politicians and 86 spouses or partners. More than

90 per cent of the people we approached agreed to be interviewed. We give more information about our research method in the Appendix.

Our perspective on the crisis confronting local government

All councillors – whether caseworkers, policymakers or managers – are at the heart of this crisis of local government. Their efforts to fulfil their public duties are met with strong official hostility and popular disdain. They have been described as 'wedded to power', as 'measuring success by the amount of money spent' and as 'prisoners of any pressure group' (Ridley 1988, p. 29). In the light of these views, we feel it is necessary to state our own position. This is based on lengthy research experience and hundreds of hours of discussion with councillors and others.

In our judgement, views such as Ridley's seriously malign elected members. Public confidence in the office of elected local councillor and in the institution of local government is being eroded in effect if not in intention. We see local government as central to the practice of democratic politics. It provides the means by which power is diffused in society. It offers the opportunity for the political system to innovate and experiment without embracing large-scale change with incalculable consequences. It recognises and can give expression to diversity and difference and allows services to be coordinated and adapted to meet the particular needs of different communities. Even the Widdicombe Committee, which seemed to many in local government to have been given the task of public prosecutor, concluded that

> the existing model of local government, although possessing many weaknesses, has great strengths. It provides for participation and openness in decision-taking. It also has the adaptability to accommodate a wide diversity of political arrangements. (Widdicombe 1986a, p. 64)

We do not believe that the social scientist can ever be completely neutral. We acknowledge that our own values have affected not only what we investigated but also how we dealt with the problems we encountered and, most obviously, our interpretations and conclusions. All three of us believe that the choice to become an elected representative, for example, should be open to any adult member of society. This is the 'official' view expressed in many Government reports and ministerial statements. But we would wish to go much further and argue that this freedom should not only exist in a legal sense but should also be a practicable option for many more people than it is at present. Where we found, for instance, that employed people or women with small children had particular difficulty in taking on a representative role we looked for solutions aimed at removing those problems rather than accepting their effective exclusion from local government.

One of the recurring themes of this book is the particular problem that women face in the world of local politics. We have tried to approach the position of women by stressing the characteristics they share with men as well as their differences. For example, women councillors are less likely to have full-time paid employment and are more likely to have considerable domestic responsibilities. Consequently, they deal with their council work differently from men in full-time jobs with few domestic obligations. We believe that employment status and family circumstances are more important determining factors than gender itself. As we suggest in later chapters, women's domestic and employment circumstances may tend to limit their self-confidence and may restrict their development of skills relevant to a political career.

The under-representation of black people on councils across the country is also of considerable concern to us. Unfortunately, their total absence from the councils within which we carried out our investigation has not allowed us to look directly at ways of increasing black recruitment, but we would urge that this question should be tackled seriously by local political parties and by those wishing to reform local government.

In terms of party politics our sympathies are diverse but in general lie more to the left than the right of the political spectrum. As the reader will see, there have been times when we could have interpreted the data in a way which might seem hostile to a political party; for example, the finding that Conservatives appear to spend less time on their council work than Liberal or Labour members is open to various interpretations. We have tried to be careful to point out these alternatives, while at the same time indicating which explanation we find more plausible given the circumstances. Nevertheless, we recognise that there might have been times when our interpretations have been affected by our political opinions. By presenting our findings fully and indicating where our sympathies lie we have tried to give the reader an opportunity to come to alternative conclusions.

PART II
THE PUBLIC WORLD

PART II

THE PUBLIC WORLD

2 Local Politicians: Ambition or Drift?

If they could find somebody better, I would not be heartbroken, as I don't really want to be a councillor . . . [but] I feel we are letting our own supporters down if we don't offer them a candidate of the party of their choice. (Monika Beaufort, Labour candidate)

Introduction

In the previous chapter, we discussed the pressures and uncertainty surrounding the role of councillors, and indicated how this reflects a long debate concerning the democratic nature of local government. The crux of this debate is whether local government is primarily a means of citizen participation rather than an instrument for the efficient delivery of national policies at the local level. These issues were raised in the discussions leading to the reorganisation in 1974, but, as we can now see, the new local government system has raised other questions of great importance; for example, the extent of involvement by political parties in the making of policy, and the decline both of independent councillors and of uncontested seats. There has also been some associated small change in the type of people recruited to councils.

In this chapter we assess the significance of these changes for the recruitment of individuals to local government. We start with an examination of the socio-economic characteristics of councillors. We then go on to look at the role of political parties in the recruitment process, before presenting a model of councillor recruitment in which individual resources, opportunities and motivations are considered together. This model is the starting point for our account of why certain individuals are more or less likely to stand as candidates and subsequently become councillors.

Who are the councillors?

The legal rules relating to local government are such that almost anyone can become a candidate. The requirements – that one is over 21, eligible to vote, and resident in the area covered by the authority for which one is standing – are easy to meet. The most significant disqualification is that candidates must not be simultaneously employed by that authority. Only a tiny proportion of adults, however, ever contest an election.

Prior to the reorganisation of local government in 1974, the total number of councillors on all types of authority (excluding parish councils) was over 40 000. In their analysis of the electoral process in local government in the early 1960s the Maud Committee observed that 'recruitment of candidates was a problem in almost all the authorities we visited' and concluded that 'in some areas it was difficult if not impossible to find sufficient people . . . . willing to accept nomination' (Maud 1967a, p. 134). In rural districts and some counties, for example, 60 per cent of seats were uncontested. In the elections of 1965, 38 per cent of councillors overall were returned unopposed (Maud 1967b, p. 45).

In recent years the situation has changed. One consequence of the reorganisation of local government in 1974 was a significant reduction in the total number of councillors to 26 000. On the face of it, this would seem to have eased the problem of finding candidates. The number of uncontested seats has certainly fallen dramatically: in the 1985 local elections virtually all the seats in shire counties were contested and the proportion of uncontested seats for other authorities in the immediately preceding period had fallen below 10 per cent. These seats were located mainly in Scotland and Wales and the more rural areas of England (Widdicombe 1986b, p. 42). This situation was also confirmed by our research: in the three county councils which we studied, there were no uncontested elections.

There is no necessary correlation, however, between the decline in the number of uncontested seats and the absolute reduction in the total number of councillors. It may be that the increased involvement of political parties at all levels of local government has been responsible for the dramatic increase in the number of contested elections (see Chapter 1, and Widdicombe 1986b, p. 23).[1] We discussed in Chapter 1 the forces that brought about the ending of consensus in local government. In the light of our discussions with councillors, we support the views of Widdicombe and others that political parties now play a dominant role in the recruitment of councillors. (Gyford *et al.* 1989) The outcome is that an electoral contest is now a normal prerequisite for entry to a council. This represents a major change in the operation of local government in many areas since the 1960s and has led to a consequent reduction in the number of independent councillors.

Is there a typical councillor?

The findings of the three main inquiries into Local Government (Maud 1967, Robinson 1977, Widdicombe 1986) are broadly in agreement that councillors, at least in respect of their socio-economic backgrounds, are unrepresentative of the population as a whole. As the Widdicombe Report claims, 'the traditional councillor stereotype is a white, middle aged, white-collar male' (1986a, p. 26). The authors of the research volume on the councillor also observed that,

> when the personal characteristics are compared across the three studies, perhaps the most remarkable aspect is the stability of the population, particularly since the Robinson Report . . . elected members as a group are still highly unrepresentative of the overall population. (Widdicombe, 1986c, p. 19)

However, in the Report, they qualify this conventional view in stating that

> overlaid on this traditional stereotype, a common perception is that the type of people who are becoming councillors is changing. There are thought to be increasing numbers of younger and female councillors . . . Our research shows that the traditional stereotype disguises a far more diverse picture in reality, and also that recent changes in the characteristics of councillors have matched popular perceptions in only a few authorities. (Widdicombe 1986a, p. 26)

Essentially, they are arguing that there still appears to be little change at the aggregate level, but that in a few local authorities members come from more diverse backgrounds. This interpretation has been confirmed in a number of recent studies including our own (Jennings 1982, Gyford 1984, Walker 1983, Barron *et al.* 1987, Bristow *et al.* 1983).

Gender

The unrepresentative nature of members is clearly seen in relation to the position of women in local politics.[2] At the time of the Maud survey only 12 per cent of all councillors were women. Their numbers had increased to 17 per cent by 1976, but in the most recent survey there was only a small further increase to 19 per cent. As the Widdicombe research makes clear, however (Widdicombe 1986c, p. 19), these figures disguise variations between types of authority and different regions in Britain. Moreover, these variations are longstanding, and similar patterns were evident in the findings of previous reports and academic research (Robinson 1977, Bristow 1980). In Wales, for example, the representation of women was much below average and particularly so in the case of Welsh counties where women constituted only 5 per cent of the total number of councillors. In Scotland, the proportion of women was also below average, except for the Scottish districts. In England the main variation is between type of authority. The highest proportion of women occurs in metropolitan districts (23 per cent), London boroughs (22 per cent) and the shire counties (21 per cent). We will look at the reasons for the under-representation of women in a later section of this chapter.

Age

The Maud Committee was also concerned with the overall age profile of councillors. At the time of their survey, in 1965, 61 per cent of female councillors and 52 per cent of male councillors were over the age of 55 and only 15 per cent of women and 21 per cent of men were below 45 years of age. These figures were grossly out of line with the age distribution of the population as a whole. Ten years later, there had only been a slight change. The proportion of men under the age of 45 had increased to 26 per cent and for women councillors to 24 per cent. Since that time, there has been no further change, so that, in 1985, approximately 50 per cent of all councillors are still over 55 years old (Widdicombe 1986c, p. 21). As with gender differences, the overall figures conceal variations between type of authority and region. For example, in the metropolitan areas, London boroughs and Scottish districts there has been, since 1976, a disproportionate increase in the number of councillors under the age of 45 (Widdicombe 1986c, p. 20, McGrew and Bristow 1983, Gyford 1984). In contrast, in the Welsh and English shire districts the number of councillors over the age of 60 has increased. As the Widdicombe researchers suggest, 'the increase in the proportion of younger councillors in the metropolitan areas would appear to explain the image of the councillor as distinctively younger than before' (1986c, p. 20) and conclude that 'the changes may be summed up as councillors as a body having become more diverse, rather than younger'.

Education

Diversity is also in evidence when we examine the educational background of councillors. Taken as a group, the evidence in all the surveys referred to in this chapter indicates that councillors spent more time at school, and that a far higher percentage received post-school education, than is the case for the population as whole and that they are far more likely to possess formal educational qualifications at every level of academic attainment. However, as the Widdicombe evidence confirms, this overall average conceals considerable divergence, and councillors in the London boroughs and the metropolitan areas are more than twice as likely to possess degrees than councillors in Wales or in English shire districts.

Employment

Turning to employment status, there has been, in recent years, a marked change, identified in the Widdicombe report, in the proportion of councillors in paid employment. This had declined since the Robinson committee reported nine years earlier, from 72 per cent to 60 per cent of all councillors. In part, this is due to a small increase in the number of unemployed councillors, but the main reason for this change is an increase in the number of retired councillors, made up principally of those taking early retirement or made redundant and no longer actively seeking paid work (Widdicombe 1986c, p. 28). Only a quarter of women councillors were in full-time paid employment, with a further sixth engaged in part-time employment. (Since neither Robinson nor Maud give separate figures for the employment of women councillors, we are unable to say whether there has been any change in this respect in recent years.) The low proportion of employed women is, as we shall argue later, almost certainly due to the particular difficulties for women in combining full-time employment with council work, (and, in many cases, family commitments as well), and not (as Bristow suggested) simply because women councillors have no 'need' of paid work because they are invariably the wives of high-earning men (Bristow, 1980).

The decline in the numbers in paid employment has not disturbed the pattern identified in previous studies that councillors are drawn disproportionately from the ranks of employers, professional and managers. Recent figures show that 41 per cent of all councillors came from these occupations compared to 14 per cent for the population as a whole (Widdicombe 1986c, p. 30). Also, only 5 per cent of councillors had a semi-skilled or un-skilled manual occupation compared to 24 per cent for the general population. (In the case of women, these data have to be treated with some caution, as in many cases they relate only to the occupational background of their husbands.) Once again, the aggregate figures disguise significant variations. In the London boroughs, English shire and metropolitan counties, and shire districts, there were a disproportionately large number of councillors with professional and managerial occupations, sometimes in excess of 50 per cent of the council. But in metropolitan districts, Welsh authorities and Scottish regions, approximately one-third of councillors came from manual occupations.

A 'new breed' of councillor

Although the general picture today in terms of gender, age, education and employment is not so different from 1976, some researchers have identified a new breed of younger councillors, many of whom are in non-manual public sector employment (Gyford 1984, Walker 1983). We have already looked at the age distribution (above) but the second point requires more discussion. Overall, the proportion of councillors employed in public sector organisations mirrors exactly the 36 per cent of the total workforce employed in this sector, but – as with occupational distribution generally – there are considerable regional variations. Some metropolitan councils and London boroughs draw up to 50 per cent of their members from the public sector, and of these over half are employed by local authorities. David Walker (1983) found that in certain inner London boroughs and the GLC, education, local government and voluntary organisations accounted for 41 per cent of those councillors in paid employment. This concentration in densely populated urban areas is – as Gyford (1984) points out – not at all surprising, given the ease of access from one's place of employment to serving as a councillor on a neighbouring authority.

In some of these authorities, also, the proportion of younger women has grown much faster than in others. These changes are related, since a high proportion of women work as teachers or other local government employees. Nevertheless, there is no authority on which the proportion of women even approaches that within the population as a whole. Gyford points out that the differences between type of authority in respect of gender, age and employment status of councillors are overlaid by party differences (Gyford *et al.* 1989). Younger members, women and those in manual occupations are found in larger numbers on councils where Labour is the majority party. In consequence, Labour councillors tend to be more representative of the population as a whole than are Conservative or Alliance[3] members.

The problem of 'twin trackers'

Those who are employed by one local authority while working voluntarily as councillors for another have been defined as 'twin trackers'[4] (Widdicombe 1986a, p. 111). Their activities have been criticised by the government and some sections of the media. In the first place it is argued that their numerical dominance on some authorities accentuates the problem of the limited range of occupations from which members are drawn, contributing further to the unrepresentative nature of some councils. Secondly, there may be a conflict of interest – which is not, incidentally, confined exclusively to local government employees – when a council member chooses to vote in accordance with the interests of his or her employing authority rather than the one she or he is nominally representing. (A rather different kind of conflict of interest, identified by the Widdicombe inquiry but of limited relevance to us here, is the position of officers who are supposedly neutral, but are politically identified by their elected membership on another authority.) Thirdly, the issue which has particularly concerned the Conservative government and other commentators in the media and elsewhere, is the amount of time these individuals are not giving to the job for which they are being paid. By implication, there is also the strong suspicion that local authorities of the same political persuasion collude with each other to allow an officer in the one to become a full-time politician in the other. This is close to the popular definition of the term 'twin trackers' which refers only to those councillors who give 'too much' time to their voluntary commitments at the expense of their paid work or otherwise abuse their dual role. This definition is clearly ideological, however, and fails to specify how much time is 'too much'; i.e. at what point is such a person abusing her/his position, and thereby, in this definition, becoming a 'twin tracker'?

Whichever definition we use, 'twin tracking' is a localised phenomenon which may occur because of the difficulties experienced by some private sector employees in obtaining sufficient time off to fulfil increasingly demanding roles as elected members in inner city authorities. Moreover, in the Widdicombe definition, this phenomenon has existed for many years. There may well be a problem in relation to widening the occupational background of council members, and in making opportunities equally open to all. The issue of 'twin tracking' has, however, been grossly exaggerated. On the Widdicombe evidence, only a minute proportion of those they define as 'twin trackers' came close to abusing their position, and there were no such individuals at all in our study. If there is a problem, however, this can best be solved by providing all employees with statutory time off sufficient to allow them to take on the demands of a council role. Moreover, to widen recruitment still further, issues such as child care and adequate remuneration for councillors have to be tackled effectively. Changes in these respects (which we look at in more detail in later chapters) could then mean that manual workers, women and the unemployed could take their place beside public sector employees and self-employed business men on local authorities throughout the country.

The turnover of councillors

The dramatic increase in contested elections, resulting from increased involvement of political parties in local government has influenced directly the rate of turnover of council membership and the continuity of members' experience on councils. Evidence collected for the Widdicombe Inquiry demonstrates that the average turnover rate of councillors between 1981 and 1985 was over 30 per cent. This evidence also reveals that between 1964 and 1985 the proportion of councillors with ten plus years of continuous service declined from 48 per cent to 35 per cent of all councillors and that the proportion with 21 years service fell from 10 per cent to 3 per cent (Widdicombe 1986c, p. 35).

The general pattern of an increased turnover of councillors disguises important variations. Gyford and his colleagues identify two types of turnover: voluntary and involuntary (Gyford *et al.* 1989). Involuntary turnover may occur at a higher rate in those authorities where 'whole council' elections occur every four years. If this happens at a time of extreme unpopularity for one of the national parties then there can be widespread change in the party composition of local councils. This, combined with the increased volatility of the electorate, means that a party may lose in excess of 50 per cent of its seats at one election, only to recover their position substantially at the next election four years later. They demonstrate that this is more likely to be the experience of councillors in the counties, Scottish authorities, London boroughs and the 60 per cent of shire districts which chose elections every four years. It is the London boroughs and the erstwhile metropolitan counties in which, in respect of the personal characteristics of members, we can identify the main differences from the general pattern of councillors described above. The emergence of younger councillors and the increased involvement of women on these councils may, therefore, in part, be explained by the vagaries of the electoral process.

Voluntary turnover, on the contrary, may occur more frequently when councillors experience increased stress from council work, or when their private commitments cannot easily be reconciled with their public ones. Factors which we found led to increased voluntary turnover include age, ill-health, the lack of time, family and domestic pressures, problems associated with paid employment and a sense of disenchantment with local government. Both the Maud and Widdicombe reports also suggest these as reasons for councillors retiring prematurely from councils; they do not, however, provide any conclusive evidence.

In many respects, the considerations councillors take into account in deciding to give up a council position are counterparts to those they and other activists advance for their decision to stand (or not) for council membership in the first place. Members contemplating retirement from a council have, however, experienced the burden of office and the consequences for other aspects of their lives, whereas those embarking on a council career are aware of the probable burden of office in general terms, but nonetheless are prepared to undertake this task. We found that both candidates and councillors were equally aware of the potential pressures of council membership, and will argue later in this chapter that entry to a council may be seen – in the main – as a process in which individuals balance a range of considerations before committing themselves to a candidature. A similar process operates when a councillor finally decides to retire from council membership.

The 'classic model' of the recruitment process

We have seen that, despite the recent changes in recruitment patterns to include people from a wider range of backgrounds, it remains true that the vast majority of councillors are still drawn from a narrow section of society. Councils are not in any respect microcosms of society as a whole. Implicit recognition of this has led some authors to conclude that in explaining political recruitment, it is sufficient merely to document the personal characteristics shared by a majority of councillors (Budge and Fairlie 1975).

Other writers have gone further and suggested that this correlation is due to unspecified 'forces' which make it more probable that people such as professionals, managers and the self-employed will succeed in becoming councillors (Stanyer 1977).

This account has laid the basis for what we describe as the 'classic' model of political recruitment. Central to this model is the claim that political activism is best seen as a movement up a hierarchy of involvement which starts with voting, moves to party membership, then to office-holding in the party and culminates in the achievement of elected office at the local or national level. It is further assumed that progress up this political ladder is inextricably linked to the individual's socio-economic status.

There is certainly evidence that an increasing number of MPs from all parties have previous experience as local councillors (Radice *et al.* 1987). This would apparently lend support to the classical model. We believe, however, that this model of political recruitment provides a partial description, only, of the end state, i.e. membership of a council. It cannot, in principle, explain the process whereby particular individuals become councillors rather than the many others who share the same personal characteristics and are equally active in political parties but who never choose to stand for a council.

Political parties and recruitment

Faced with this dilemma, some commentators have argued that it is necessary to go beyond a consideration of the socio-economic status of activists and explore the role of political parties in the recruitment process (Brand 1973, Dearlove 1979, Bochel 1966). In their view, the parties, in their selection of candidates, open up opportunities for a few and close off opportunities for others. Furthermore, these writers assume that, in making their choice of candidate, the party selectors have in mind a list of qualities which would characterise the ideal recruit, and only those who measure up to this ideal will be selected. Where such 'ideal' candidates fail to present themselves, the selectors will actively try to recruit people with the relevant qualities but, in the absence of suitable prospective candidates, may be obliged to compromise.

We found, however, that the reality is rather different: it is very common for party selectors to be faced with very few, if any, individuals willing to come forward as candidates. The 'compromise' candidate may therefore be more common than the 'ideal' one, and the 'selection' process, in consequence, provides little or no scope for choice by party selectors.

Different parties respond to this situation in different ways. The Conservative Party, as a number of writers have observed, is quite willing to accept non-party members as candidates so long as they demonstrate some voluntary activity in the local community (Brand 1973, Collins 1978a). In a study of councillor recruitment in Glasgow, Brand noted that the Progressive (anti-socialist) Party would recruit promising individuals who were not members of the party (Brand 1973). Our research endorses this finding: in our discussions with both candidates and councillors we met a number of Conservative Party candidates who achieved their candidature before joining the party. In contrast, selectors in the Labour Party are more concerned to secure candidates who have served a period of apprenticeship in the party. They are, however, also frequently faced with a shortage of candidates and find it necessary to exert considerable pressure on party activists to ensure a full slate of candidates at local elections. In this situation the qualities of the candidates take second place to the tactical judgement that it is necessary for the party to fight in all wards.

Our findings, along with the evidence of other studies, therefore confront directly the allegation that party selectors have a bias in favour of certain categories of people and are particularly prejudiced against women. In our view, the notion that discrimination occurs at the selection stage runs counter to the general picture of local parties struggling to find sufficient numbers of party activists willing to stand as candidates at local elections.

Motivation and recruitment

Any analysis of political recruitment which focuses simply on socio-economic status or the role of selectors can provide only a partial understanding of a most complex process. All the studies referred to above suffer from the limitation that they focus on one or at most two aspects of the recruitment process. This may provide some necessary factual information but does not enhance our understanding of the recruitment process as a whole. A particular weakness is that they do not examine the councillor's own perception of the factors influencing her or his decision to stand as a candidate. They therefore ignore or take for granted individual motivations, and fail even to consider the reasons why a majority of 'suitable' people do not even contemplate seeking public office.

The importance of motivation was acknowledged in a somewhat limited study conducted for the Maud Committee more than twenty years ago. The interviewers approached a sample of councillors with the preamble, 'it would be useful to know how you yourself became a councillor'. They immediately followed this up, however, with a series of specific probes asking councillors to respond to a preconceived set of alternative motives. In effect, they were making assumptions concerning the probable factors influencing recruitment, largely ignoring the councillor's own interpretation of their situation at the time they decided to become candidates. They were also attempting to categorise motivation in isolation from the social, political and institutional context in which it develops.

A more fruitful starting point to the study of recruitment is to follow Gordon's model (Gordon 1979). He argued that an adequate explanation must incorporate three essential considerations: individual resources, including social position and skills; the opportunities available, including the nature of the party and electoral systems, and the party selection process; and personal motivations such as ambition, expectations and attitudes towards the perceived costs of council membership. Although analytically distinct, these dimensions are each conditioned by the others (Barber 1965).

An alternative approach

While in principle endorsing Gordon's model, we feel it is necessary to employ rather broader definitions of the concepts of resources, motivations and opportunities than Gordon proposed. For example, those writers who have focused on socio-economic factors are essentially looking at one kind of resource. We would wish to add to this any attribute which enables an individual to attain a desired goal: for example, experience, self-confidence and relevant skills, which may be acquired in party and community activity, or family activities, as well as those derived from their education and employment.

We also adopt a broader interpretation of opportunities than that discussed by Gordon and see opportunities of two kinds: first the opportunities provided by the parties in their selection procedures; secondly the opportunities individuals provide for themselves, by being in the right place at the right time (or, in the case of the reluctant candidates, the wrong place at the wrong time).

Finally, we look at motivations, as reported to us by the individuals themselves.

This more integrated approach became evident to us during our initial research into councillors' perceptions of the relationship between their public and private worlds, and we developed it in our subsequent study of the recruitment of women candidates. Many of the data in this chapter therefore refer directly to women's recruitment but we have indicated the relevance to men at appropriate points.

Why do they do it?

As we have indicated, a major lacuna in the literature on political recruitment relates to the dimensions of individual motivations. In view of this, we decided to ask political activists (councillors, candidates and non-candidates) a series of deliberately open-ended questions regarding their decision to stand – or not – for their local council. We received a wide variety of responses, of which the following are examples:

> I'm not the sort of person to be able to sit back if I don't agree with what's going on. I can't just sit back and do nothing, I have to become involved. (Daphne Herriott, Conservative candidate and town councillor)

> Mrs Carlisle asked me if I would stand for selection. I didn't think I was ready. There may come a time . . . But I didn't feel I was ready then, I hadn't thought about it enough. (Audrey Lightfoot, Conservative Party member and non-candidate)

At the time, my branch was rather small and it took me three months to decide whether I'd do it or not – with very little confidence, I might add . . . I know what I wanted to do, and what I wanted to change, but I didn't really know that [the council] was the avenue I wanted to do it through. (Pauline Smith, Labour backbencher)

How can we make sense of these various reactions? In our view, these responses suggest a subtle interplay between the resources available to them, the opportunities open to them and personal motivations and intentions. Our general conclusion was that candidature was not necessarily a deliberate or consciously worked-for objective, as the classic model would lead us to expect, but nor was it strictly an 'accidental' outcome. Borrowing from Matza, we see this as a process of drift, 'a gradual process of movement, largely unperceived by the actor', the outcome of which may at any stage be accidental or unpredictable (Matza 1964, p. 29). Some individuals who eventually become councillors engage initially in sporadic community activity, may become party members, hold party office and stand for an unwinnable seat before successfully contesting a local election. For these people, the final decision to stand for election may be seen as the culmination of an extended process which commences long before the formal selection stage. There is, however, no inevitability about this progression. People may drift between activity and inactivity. Some individuals may move to candidature, others may strongly resist, whereas others again may be catapulted on to the council with little or no prior involvement in party politics.

Moreover, we found that an individual's identity as an activist was often unclear and changeable. There was no clear distinction between councillors, candidates (some of whom subsequently became councillors) and non-candidates; and indeed, as it turned out, some of the declared non-candidates became candidates soon after our interview. Some candidates – having been persuaded merely to fly the flag for their party – had no real intention of becoming councillors and felt it would be personally disastrous if they were elected. On the other hand some of our non-candidates fully intended standing as candidates at some later date, and were, in effect, more serious potential councillors than some of those who were currently standing.

Resources

Political awareness and self-confidence are part of our wider definition of 'resources'. These may stem from being brought up in a politically active household which, in turn, may have the effect of broadening an individual's understanding of the political process and enhancing political skills, which may lead to a desire for a political career. Previous researchers have recognised the importance of this factor in disposing people to activism, but have not defined it specifically as a political resource. Both Maud (1967) and Budge and his colleagues (Budge *et al.* 1972) found that at least 50 per cent of councillors came from politically active backgrounds. Our work suggests that, whereas only a quarter of councillors and candidates in our studies came from such backgrounds, a substantial majority nonetheless claimed to come from families where there was a 'keen interest' in politics and where political events were 'frequently discussed'. In itself, this may be sufficient to enhance an individual's self-confidence to engage in political dialogue and this may lead to the development of effective political communication.

The acquisition of such skills does not, of course, mean that such individuals will necessarily embark on a political career. In our study, for example, non-candidates were more likely than candidates to come from households where some relatives were politically active in local government. The demands of employment or family life, or the lack of opportunity or absence of any real motivation may well offset any resource advantage. It is, however, noteworthy that women were much more likely than men to stress the need for a longstanding interest in politics. We suggest that women who persist in their political activism in the face of obstacles unlikely to be experienced by men may perhaps need more resources (including self-confidence) and more determination than men, in similar circumstances.

Self-confidence as a resource

Many of the councillors and candidates we talked to emphasised the importance of self-confidence. This is developed in a number of ways. For example, those from a professional and managerial background who have experienced higher education are more likely to feel confident in their ability or skills to complete certain tasks such as chairing meetings, writing reports and raising issues. This self-assurance may then be reinforced by their involvement in the decision-making process where they work. On the other hand, many women do not have the kind of work experience which can enhance their self-confidence; and those who have withdrawn from employment (albeit temporarily) are also less likely to continue to share this degree of self-confidence.

> I find it hard to talk, not to individuals but to groups of people. I think that's something women find in general, just standing up and talking to a group of people is very hard. I can do it, but I don't think I do it well, and I don't enjoy it at all. (Lucy Waite, Labour non-candidate)

> A lot of women we've asked, their self-image doesn't include being a councillor. They actually have to be told, 'You'd be a good one.' (Nancy Dixon, Liberal Chair)

> I had been interested, but to be quite honest, I didn't really . . . feel I had the nerve or the confidence to do it . . . . My first reaction was, 'What, me? No, never!' (Myra Green, Liberal candidate)

We believe that, more than anything else, it is this lack of self-confidence which explains the under-representation of women on many local authorities, and, conversely, the predominance of (white) male professionals. It is not, as we have said earlier, that party selectors discriminate against women; nor do we accept Bristow's claim that a high level of affluence explains the higher than average proportion of women on some councils. While superficially correct, this is in no sense an explanation, and there are serious flaws to his argument. The socio-economic data on which he was drawing relate to male occupations only; therefore, any implications for women members of that authority must, at best, be extremely tentative. Many of the wives of businessmen have relatively few resources on their own account, particularly if they have not been employed for many years, and have few educational qualifications (Barron 1989).

Employment as a resource

While it is true that a majority of Conservative women councillors were non-employed 'housewives' married to professional and managerial partners, the same may be said of many other women who share many of the same attributes but who do not embark on a political career.

Moreover, many Labour and Liberal members did not conform to this pattern at all. Many of them were taking a break of a few years from a professional career while their children were young. Others tried, with difficulty, to combine paid employment with a council career. Many of those who were non-employed bemoaned the loss of income and the expense of council work (see Chapter 6). On the Labour side, certainly, the proportion of women who neither 'needed' to take paid work nor wanted to do so was minimal. Nor, in our view, was this necessarily a disadvantage to them, since it is through occupational experience that people (women and men) often gain useful resources, including self-confidence. It is in our view this which helps to explain the predominance of white middle-class males both on local councils and in parliament.

Where resources of any kind – educational attainment, voluntary group involvement, or work experience – build up in a cumulative manner, an individual will feel increasingly able to engage in political action of some kind. (This is not to say that they *will* do so.) Conversely, where class, gender, race or occupational experience limit resources (as they do particularly for women) those individuals are less likely to acquire that minimal level of self-confidence which is a necessary (if not sufficient) prerequisite for embarking on a political career.

Opportunities

Whatever resources the individual possesses, she or he may still not have the opportunity to embark on a political career. Women, in particular, are therefore in a 'Catch-22' situation. Non-employed women whose children are grown up are likely to have both time and opportunity to devote to council work, but, as we have seen, may have relatively few resources, and if they have been out of the job market for some time, may lack self-confidence. Those in employment may in principle be more confident and possess relevant skills (and therefore have some of the required resources to stand for the council) but they are often faced with undertaking the main burden of family care in addition to their paid jobs (Mansfield and Collard 1988, Oakley 1974 and 1976; see Chapter 4 for further discussion). They may therefore find it more difficult than non-employed women to combine their existing commitments with a political career. That some of them nevertheless do so is an indication of the strength of their motivation and persistence. The question therefore becomes not 'Why so few women?' but, given the factors working against them, 'Why are there are so many?' (Stacey and Price 1981).

Most previous commentators have concentrated on the opportunities provided by political parties through their selection procedures. As we have seen, however, any selection process relies on the availability of individuals who put themselves in a position where they may be selected. Within the total pool of potential candidates – which is almost the entire local electorate – there is that very small minority who, by joining and actively involving themselves in a political party or other voluntary organisations, show themselves able and willing to take on the larger task of local representative; i.e. they have, in one sense, put themselves in a position where they may be considered for a candidature.

Although the councillors and candidates in our studies did not always distinguish these two kinds of opportunity, the two-sided nature of the selection process is implicit in their comments. If party membership is the starting point for creating an opportunity then a high proportion of candidates and councillors do place themselves in a position where they will be invited to stand. A majority have been active members of their parties for some years prior to candidature and many explained their recruitment in terms of a development from these activities. While this apparently confirms the classic model of political recruitment, and may have some relevance in explaining the political activities of Labour members in particular, it is far less apposite in explaining the recruitment of Conservative and Alliance candidates. In both these parties, as we saw earlier, candidates are frequently recruited from amongst non-party members, and selectors in the Conservative Party, in particular, are quite likely to invite non-members who are active in voluntary organisations to stand as candidates, as the following comment illustrates:

> It really wasn't my idea in the beginning, you know. I wasn't aching to get into public life. But I was actually, after the initial few minutes [after he approached me], interested . . . . If I didn't get in, I would in fact join the [party] committee for this ward because I think they do a terrific support job . . . . I was the sort of dregs at the bottom of the barrel, they were desperate! (Linda Taplow, Conservative candidate)

In the case of the Labour Party where the selection process tends to be more formal, and requires a shortlist made up of established party members, the party also faces considerable difficulty in many areas in finding candidates. In consequence, considerable effort is expended to persuade or cajole party members to stand for election. The result is that many individuals 'volunteer' in circumstances where there are no readily available alternative candidates.

> There was nobody else! They were all sitting there saying, 'Who's going to do it this year?' Edna did it last year and she said, 'I'm not going to do it . . .'. (Emily Poole, Labour candidate)

For the majority of candidates and councillors the idea that they should stand for election was suggested by others, usually by party members. These party members are thereby offering to other members the opportunity to become candidates. Nevertheless, each individual, in becoming a party activist, is to some extent also helping to provide that opportunity for her or himself. In this respect, the opportunity is created jointly by party selectors and those who allow themselves to be selected.

Council work offered a rather different kind of opportunity to some married women who, having given up employment to care for their families, were looking for an interesting and challenging activity outside the home. Many of these were Labour and Liberal members who were willing to become councillors for one term only before returning to paid work. Other older women whose partners were employed in professional or managerial positions could perhaps more easily than other people afford the additional expense of council work, and neither wanted nor needed to earn a wage themselves. These women, who were more likely to delay their decision to become candidates until their children had left home, were predominately Conservative party members.

Motivations

We have said that the classical model takes motivations for granted. Implicit in this model is the idea of some clear personal ambition on the part of potential candidates; that is, that they actively want to become councillors. Our study, however, does not entirely support this interpretation. The evidence from our own research and other studies strongly suggests that very few candidates are 'self-starters' in the sense that they have a clear ambition to become a local councillor and plan the route accordingly. Instead, the step from party or voluntary group activity to candidature often seems to be taken without much preparation. There is remarkably little evidence of burning ambition and most of those who accept the invitation – unlike those who resist the offer – do so reluctantly because they do not wish to let the party down.

> The sitting member decided to stand down, and it was really – I hadn't planned to be a councillor but people in the branch were putting pressure on me and saying 'We'd like you to stand', and it was sort of a culmination . . . . (Sarah Hibbert, Labour Chair)

In spite of differences in their experiences, however, neither Sarah Hibbert nor Linda Taplow (whom we quoted earlier, p. 48) initially saw herself as the right person for the job, but each was persuaded by others to stand when no alternative candidates were available. There is some evidence from both our own and other studies, that women are more likely than men to need to be persuaded to stand for public office (Skar, 1981, Means 1971). Men also, however, pointed out that they had needed considerable persuasion to take on council work:

> The local party [wherever I lived] always coerced me into going . . . . I've always been approached . . . . I didn't intend to go on. (Leonard Wilson, Conservative councillor)

While councillors could often recall that they were asked to stand, and by whom, their reasons for going ahead were usually couched in terms of public issues, and often involved a sense of moral obligation or social pressure. The most frequently cited reason for becoming a candidate was to assist the local party in the absence of any other suitable or willing individual. As we have seen, this is related to the question of opportunities, and it seems that the motivation here is an unwillingness to disappoint one's colleagues in the party.

> The secretary asked me if I would stand . . . . He said, you won't get in, but we've got to have somebody here. I said, well, I'll have a try. (Dora Charles, Conservative candidate; see also Emily Poole, above, p. 48).

Other councillors were motivated by a concern to care for the local community and believed that people with local knowledge should be involved in local policy-making. Some also referred to specific issues such as education or the provision of local amenities as the reason for their involvement in local politics.

> I wanted to do something for local people and thought I had something to offer. (Pat Curry, Labour candidate)

> I decided to try to become a county councillor because I was absolutely appalled at the state of the town. (Eleanor Mansfield, Liberal backbencher)

Many candidates and councillors commented in general terms that the burdens of domestic life, which bear more heavily on women than men, might explain the under-representation of women on councils. Surprisingly, however, they did not see this as a significant factor in their own particular case. Nevertheless, they did acknowledge their need for a supportive partner (who was perhaps able to take on some of the domestic burden – see Chapter 4) many of them emphasising that, without this support, their current level of political activity would be impossible.

Very few indeed presented their initial involvement in terms of ideological commitment or ambition. This is consistent with the view that only a minority of activists give high priority to

ideological issues and that personal experience and social influences are far more important (Stack 1970, Rose 1962, Bochel 1966,
Gyford 1984).

The only mention of any ideological perspective was from those
women who felt the need to put forward a 'women's viewpoint' in
contrast to the predominant male view of the existing council; and
a very few people who wanted to resolve a particular issue, or
'change society' generally. Others, however, had more personal
reasons for standing, but normally they could not explain them any
more clearly than by saying simply, they wanted to become
councillors, or it was the 'right time' for them now:

> I suppose I thought, well, the time's right, I'll do it . . . . Let's
> say I'm getting older and perhaps the more active avenues that
> I've been pursuing, perhaps I've gone over to being not quite so
> active. (Doreen Peel, Conservative candidate)

Some people suggested that women and men tended to have
different reasons for standing for the council. Whereas women only
did so if they had fairly clear objectives which they wished to fulfil,
men – in their view – were more likely to see it as the next
inevitable step, and take it without much thought or because they
were taken with the image or the status of becoming a councillor.
These remarks, however, were mostly made by *women* about *other*
prospective candidates or councillors, and there was no indication
from councillors or candidates themselves that issues of status or
prestige had great importance for them.

Why NOT be a councillor?

The other side of motivation concerns the people who do *not* want
to be councillors: why is this? What reasons did our non-candidates
give for turning down repeated requests that they stand for the
local council? Reasons fell into four main categories. Firstly there
were those (a minority) who cited family reasons, such as the age of
their children or their partner's refusal to countenance it. Secondly,
and often related to family-centred reasons, were reasons relating
to lack of time, or the need to give up other activities if they were
to take on additional commitments. Thirdly, there were those who

criticised the councillor role, or certain aspects of it, and did not like the necessity of representing a particular party and toeing the party line. Finally, many women, in particular, felt they lacked the necessary qualities to become effective councillors. Some of them simply said they did not want to do it, whereas others said they were not 'front' people, could not give speeches, or lacked experience or self-confidence:

> I find it quite confusing at times. If it was just to be mainly practical things, that would be a piece of cake, but I find it very difficult actually to speak at meetings . . . . I think it's lack of confidence, to be honest. (Margaret Wilson, Labour activist)

This therefore returns us back to the dimension of 'resources' with which we started.

In the light of this evidence, we believe there is a distinction between those who take on the role of candidate or councillor, who give 'public' reasons for doing so, or at least for failing to resist the pressure to stand; and those who *do* resist, who are more likely to give private and personal reasons relating either to their family circumstances, their lack of time, or their personal qualities and lack of experience.

Conclusion

In our view, the classical model of political recruitment is too simple, though elements of it are present in many cases. Extensive party experience is neither necessary nor sufficient for council membership, but it makes a candidature more likely, and the association is certainly stronger for Labour Party activists. As we have seen, however, a significant number of Conservatives are catapulted into a candidature and thereby into council membership without any prior 'apprenticeship' in their parties. In all parties, there are people who are nudged reluctantly into taking on a candidature. If, against their own expectations, they are elected, then the notion of 'drift' we referred to earlier is not wide of the mark. Those who drift are seen by selectors as suitable prospective candidates, and fail to resist the moral pressure to stand. In contrast, other equally suitable potential candidates with considerable experience and enthusiasm for party activism, nevertheless stand firm in their decision to remain as activists outside the council chamber. This resistance may take different forms and operate at different stages in the recruitment process. Some of the candidates we interviewed could be regarded as having drifted into candidature, but they had allowed this to happen in the knowledge that the seat they were contesting was not, realistically, winnable for their party.

We believe that drift and resistance may be seen as opposite reactions to pressure from fellow activists and selectors. That is, when the opportunity to stand for a council is presented to them, drifters acquiesce, albeit reluctantly, but resisters stand firm in their refusal. This may be, in some cases, because they lack any real motivation to become councillors; in other cases, it may be that their assessment of their own qualities convinces them, even in the face of considerable pressure, that they must persist in their refusal. In a rather different position are those who positively want and actively seek out an opportunity to stand for a candidacy. The classic model, notwithstanding its lack of a motivational perspective, perhaps best fits this pattern, which we term the 'intender' approach.

All three types – the drifter, the resister and the intender – are characterised primarily by their contrasting motivations. It is, however, important to be aware of the dimensions of resources and opportunities which provide the context in which motivations must be considered. For example, it is only those with sufficient resources in a situation of opportunity of whom a response – either to drift or resist – will be demanded. Some intenders fail to become selected as candidates in local council elections for lack of opportunity.

The decision to stand is easier for those whose paid employment is flexible, is not a significant or enjoyable part of their lives, and is not – as is the case for some married women councillors – seen as essential for financial survival. With regard to women also, council membership may be easier for those who have neither partners nor children, or whose partners share their ideological beliefs. However, family and employment situations, important though they are, are not the sole deciding factors.

Nor is wanting to become a councillor enough in itself: several women who wanted very much to be selected were not selected –

though in most cases we do not believe this was due to deliberate bias and on the face of it we see no reason why men should not, on occasion, be in a similar position. Others, who were successful in becoming candidates were not elected; nor, because of the area in which they lived, was there much chance of their obtaining a winnable seat in future. Others were deterred from doing what they wanted to do by their partners who made it clear that becoming a councillor would not be welcomed. This, we feel, is less likely to deter men, who will carry on regardless of their partner's misgivings, and, in most cases, will be able to ensure sufficient tacit support to do so.

In contrast, others, both men and women, were indifferent or even mildly hostile to the idea of standing for the council, but ended up with a seat because of outside pressures. That many of these reluctant recruits later made excellent councillors fulfilling their role efficiently and conscientiously and gaining considerable satisfaction from so doing is to their credit rather than to that of a system which provides so little official encouragement to our locally elected and voluntary council members.

Notes

1. Evidence presented to the Widdicombe committee demonstrates that 83 per cent of all candidates are party members and that over 30 per cent of independents are also members of political parties. Gyford *et al.* (1989) suggest that in 1987, 90 per cent of councillors were party members.
2. Ethnic minorities also appear to be significantly under-represented and particularly so in areas where they constitute a sizeable proportion of the local community, but there are no reliable data.
3. As they then were.
4. This definition is to some extent at odds with the popular use of the term.

3 Can Local Politicians Cope?

You've got a phone that's red hot . . . (Mrs Pearson, wife of Labour backbencher).

Introduction

In the previous chapter we described the pathways through which a small minority of citizens become elected representatives. Whether or not councillors drift into office or achieve membership of a local authority as a result of a clearly-defined intention, they will face many varied and conflicting demands on their time and energies. In responding to (and often encouraging) these demands, they are influenced by the 'public' world of the council chamber and party group, the private world of family relationships, leisure and employment and the expectations that they bring to the task.

In this chapter we look at different aspects of the response that councillors make to these demands. By looking at previous literature as well as our own data, we attempt to answer what, at first sight, appears to be an uncontentious question: What is the workload of the councillor? Our evidence demonstrates that the average member's council and council-related workload is around twice as great as previous studies have suggested. We then examine the attitudes of members and their partners to the work they do and how they cope with a diverse and extensive range of tasks. Finally, we explore how councillors adapt to the pressures they and their partners face and how these shape members' different political styles.

The workload of the councillor: the official view

The past three decades have seen three separate official inquiries which have attempted to answer the question: What is the workload of the councillor? In terms of the hours spent on council and council-related business in a 'typical' month the results of these inquiries can be stated very simply: 52 hours (1964); 79 hours (1976); and 74 hours (1985) (Maud 1967, Robinson 1977, Widdicombe 1986a). These figures suggest that since the 1960s there has been a substantial increase in the hours worked by members followed by a slight decline.

The most recent data are those produced for the Widdicombe inquiry on the conduct of local authority business. As one would expect there were marked variations around the average of 74 hours per month. More time was spent by councillors on upper-rather than lower-tier authorities, and in Scotland and Wales rather than in England. Within England more time was spent in the metropolitan rather than shire areas. At the extremes Scottish regional and islands councillors spent 129 hours per month as against 58 by English shire district councillors.

Labour councillors put in an average of 92 hours a month while the average Liberal and Conservative councillor put in 68 hours.The unemployed spent more time (105 hours) than those in paid employment (67 hours). Office holders (for example committee Chairs) devoted an average of 80 hours a month while the backbencher (without office) devoted 64 hours. Those over the age of 60 spent more time (81 hours) than those who were younger (71 hours).

Most of the time was spent on council and committee meetings (21 hours per month) or in related preparation (18 hours) and travel (7 hours). The time spent by councillors on constituency matters and dealing with pressure groups was 13 hours per month.

Are these figures valid?

We have many reservations concerning the validity of this evidence. Firstly, the three surveys are not fully comparable. The initial inquiry (Maud) failed to ask councillors about the time they spent in such activities as party meetings related to council work and in public consultation. The second inquiry (Robinson) omitted to ask councillors about the latter of these two activities. Secondly, the fieldwork for the Robinson and Widdicombe inquiries was undertaken at times which were, arguably, atypical in terms of workload. The survey for the Robinson committee was carried out soon after local government reorganisation when councillors' activities might have been temporarily inflated during the initial years of the new authorities. The Widdicombe committee's survey was conducted during the summer of 1985 – a time of year, as the researchers state, 'when council business is likely to be both reduced and obviously affected by holidays and by the summer recess' (Widdicombe 1986c, p. 41).

There is, thirdly, a more fundamental reason for doubting these figures. These three surveys were based upon postal questionnaires sent out to a sample (typically 10 per cent) of councillors. Postal surveys – although cheap to administer – have a number of serious drawbacks; in particular, their low response rate, ambiguities in interpreting questions, lack of opportunities to probe answers and the necessarily limited nature of the questions which can be asked. These surveys illustrate these shortcomings. The Widdicombe inquiry achieved only a 61 per cent response rate; almost 900 councillors failed to reply. In all three surveys researchers asked councillors about a 'typical' or 'average' month. This form of questioning, we suggest, is likely to lead to a wide variety of interpretations and considerable inaccuracies.

In addition to the questionnaire sent to a sample of councillors, the Widdicombe Committee commissioned a survey in which 550 councillors and officers were questioned in person on a range of issues. The aim was to supplement the quantitative data from the postal questionnaire and to gain an appreciation of the more complex and subtle qualitative factors which underlie the operation of local authorities. The researchers reported that in 85 per cent of the authorities which were visited, the balance of opinion was that the time required of councillors or actually being put in had increased in recent years. There were few, if any, suggestions that council work required less time spent on it than at some time in the recent past (Widdicombe 1986b, p. 51).

The Committee was, therefore, faced with apparently conflicting data: the results of the postal survey indicated that workloads had decreased but the qualitative data from the interview survey indicated that they had increased. Such a conflict did not trouble the Committee. Without weighing the evidence it concluded that:

There is no clear evidence to support the commonly held view that councillors are devoting increasing amounts of time to council work. This was certainly the perception of councillors and officers interviewed in the course of our study of the political organisation of authorities [the interview survey]. But the view is not supported when information provided by councillors themselves in response to our sample [postal] questionnaire survey. (Widdicombe 1986a, p. 28)

In this manner the Committee abruptly dismissed, without discussion or justification, the findings of the interview survey. Indeed, had it provided a justification it would have undermined its heavy reliance on the interview survey in other ways. Yet, given the nature of the questions in the postal survey, on which the supposedly 'hard' data relating to work hours were based, we find the Committee's cavalier treatment of this contradictory evidence very hard to understand. In the next section, we will consider the appropriate form of questioning to elicit both valid and reliable data on councillors' workhours.

Our approach

As we have said, the postal surveys sent out by these inquiries asked councillors about a 'typical' week or month. Our previous research experience coupled with a small trial we carried out as part of a larger study suggested that any notion of a 'typical' week or month was likely to be highly imprecise and to vary according to the time of year and from member to member. In addition, councillors' memories of past events and their duration was also likely to be variable and, to some degree, inaccurate. The best that could be hoped for was for a reasonable estimate for the time put in, and, at worst, the researchers would be given an answer which was pure speculation.

We therefore decided in our study to question county councillors on particular activities undertaken on specific and recent dates. We also had the advantage of personal interviews which allowed probing and memory jogging where this seemed appropriate.

Accordingly, we used two methods to measure the workload of the county councillors. Firstly, we asked councillors to go through their own diaries for the last two complete weeks preceding the interview, and to tell us from that information, and assisted by memory, what meetings and other commitments they had actually attended during that period. We called this method the Recall. Secondly, we asked councillors to record for us in as much detail as possible, all incidents, activities and events – both public and private – for one subsequent week. We provided them with a specially printed Diary for this purpose. We hoped that respondents would record incidents as they happened: for example, phone calls or informal conversations with constituents or officers. In that way we hoped we would get a more complete record of those activities which – though making considerable demands on the individual concerned – were not recorded as formal appointments in their diaries and were often not remembered a week or so later.

It is notable that the Maud Committee would have preferred to use a similar method:

> Ideally, we should have liked councillors to keep a diary for us over an adequate period of time, and to record in detail all the public activities they carried out and how much time they spent on them. (Maud, Vol. II, p. 89).

Presumably the Widdicombe inquiry, like the Maud Committee, decided such a method was impracticable. Had it used the 'diary' method it might have come to very different conclusions. In our experience it is possible to collect reliable data by these means. Very few respondents found it unacceptably time-consuming and 54 out of 62 councillors were able to complete their Diaries.

Some councillors told us that the chosen weeks were not typical in some way – for example, they had been ill (and therefore had done less than usual) or a particular event like a fund-raising garden fête or a local government conference had meant that the selected week had been a particularly busy one. We felt, however, that these irregularities would tend to balance each other out, and that any over- or underestimates resulting from this would be smaller than the error which would result from a generalised recall of a 'typical' month.

The workhours of county councillors

We received Recall information from 61 and Diaries from 54 of the councillors we interviewed. In almost every case, the hours recorded in the Diary were considerably more than those reported in the Recall, commonly being between one-and-a-half and two-and-a-half times as much. From Recall information, the mean average hours reported by councillors was 20.7 per week (equivalent to slightly more than 82 hours per month). On the basis of the Diary information, this average rose to 34.2 per week (or nearly 137 hours per month).

These figures conceal considerable variations: the highest Recall figure was 57.5 per week and the lowest was 2.5 hours; the highest and lowest Diary figures were 62 and seven hours respectively.

As can be seen in Table 3.1, leading councillors, for example, Chairs of committees, had higher than average workloads. Labour and Liberal councillors put in rather more hours than Conservatives and women councillors reported more hours than men.

TABLE 3.1   Councillors' mean workhours per week by council position, party and gender

	RECALL		DIARY	
Backbenchers	15.9	(29 cllrs)	29.4	(25 cllrs)
Chairs	25.3	(32 cllrs)	38.4	(29 cllrs)
Conservative	20.5	(22 cllrs)	28.9	(19 cllrs)
Labour	22.7	(30 cllrs)	37.6	(28 cllrs)
Liberal	15.5	(9 cllrs)	34.8	(7 cllrs)
Men	18.6	(31 cllrs)	30.8	(27 cllrs)
Women	23.1	(30 cllrs)	37.6	(27 cllrs)

The consistent difference between the Recall and the Diary figures indicates that the exclusive reliance placed by official inquiries in earlier years on postal questionnaires is unjustified and confirms the unsatisfactory nature of that type of survey which we mentioned earlier in this chapter. The average workload as reflected in the Diaries, 137 hours a month, is considerably in excess of the 101 hours reported for English shire county councillors in the postal survey done for the Widdicombe committee (Widdicombe 1986c, p. 43). This strongly suggests that councillors' workloads are very much higher than has been officially recognised to date. Moreover, the respective figures for backbenchers and chairs lends support to the suggestion that the gap between them (compared to the 1976 survey for the Robinson committee) is if anything narrowing rather than widening (Widdicombe 1986c, p. 43). Finally, and most significantly, a clear gender difference is apparent. Women, on average, spent 20 per cent more time on council work than men. One other academic study has shown a similar difference, (Martlew *et al.* 1985, Martlew 1988, p. 59), but no official study has analysed councillors' activities in terms of gender.

We do not claim that the figures 'typify' in some way the average councillor and wish to emphasise that the data are based on information from 61 county councillors from three county councils only. We feel, however, that they should be taken seriously at least as an indication of the likely burden of work in these three local authorities. Moreover, we are not aware that these authorities were particularly atypical of many other councils which have similar characteristics of party control and degree of urbanisation; nor do our data have the weaknesses of the Widdicombe survey which was, as we stated earlier, carried out in the summer recess of that year. The week which was the basis of the Diary was usually at least a month later than the two-week period reported in the Recall. In many cases the interval between these two 'snapshots' was even greater. We are confident, therefore, of the representative character of the periods covered by our survey.

We believe the data we have reported strongly support two propositions: firstly, that councillors' workloads are very much higher than has hitherto been officially recognised; and secondly, that there is very great diversity in how members define and execute their roles as elected representatives.

The composition of councillors' workloads

We analysed councillors' workloads, in both the Recall and the Diary, in terms of the following seven categories:

1   Council and committee meetings.
2   Travel time
3   Party group meetings
4   Other party meetings
5   Meetings with voluntary bodies and pressure groups
6   Other meetings
7   Other activities

With the exception of our first category (council and committee meetings), none of these corresponds exactly to the subdivisions used in previous surveys. 'Travel time', for example, in our inquiry includes *all* travel which was necessary to fulfil the role as defined by the councillor. It included travel to and from the constituency which the councillor represented and travel to party meetings. The earlier inquiries, on the other hand, were interested only in travel to and from council and committee meetings.

Our 'other meetings' category is rather larger than that used in the other studies because we felt that it would be difficult to distinguish meetings attended as official council representatives from those attended for other reasons. We were also interested in the wider activities of councillors and, therefore, asked about all kinds of party activities and meetings and not just party group meetings. Since most councillors nowadays (and all those in our study) are the official candidates of a political party, we felt that most of them would see a certain minimum of party involvement as an essential element of their role. The failure of the Widdicombe survey to make use of this category sits uneasily with the claim in the Committee's Report that its recommendations are 'attuned . . . to political reality . . .' (Widdicombe 1986a, p. 57).

Finally, our 'other activities' category is very diverse. It includes preparation time, casework (including phone calls), attendance at conferences, discussions with officers, and so on. This category has the largest discretionary or 'self-generating' element.

Figure 3.1 shows the composition of councillors' workloads as they were reflected in the Recall and Diary. It confirms the findings of the earlier surveys that council meetings (for which members are entitled to receive an attendance allowance) comprise a relatively small element (about four hours a week) in the total workload. Furthermore, for this category, there is no significant difference between the hours in the Recall and those in the Diary. In contrast, however, Diary time spent on 'other activities' was more than 14 hours a week – more than twice that of the Recall. It indicates that this varied category accounts for the greater part of the difference, which we referred to earlier in this chapter, between the total workload in the Recall and that in the Diary. Political party activities are covered in categories 3 (Party group meetings) and 4 (other party meetings). These figures confirm those in the Widdicombe survey. Interestingly, and possibly in contrast to the perceptions of the media and some electors, these activities do not appear very time-consuming. The notion of councillors as being involved in interminable party group meetings appears distant from reality. More surprisingly, at a time when there has been much discussion about the relationship of members with organisations outside the council (see Chapter 1), it is clear that meetings with voluntary groups and pressure groups are the least significant activities for councillors.

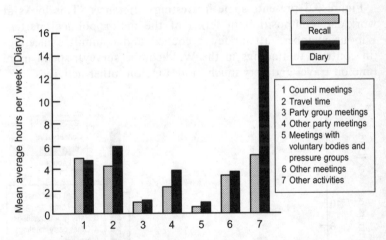

FIGURE 3.1   Councillors' workloads: Recall and Diary

Gender is the focus of the analysis in Figure 3.2 which is based on the Diary data alone. This suggests that the difference between the total workloads of female and male councillors (referred to earlier in this chapter) is explained by women members reporting higher loads in virtually all activities.

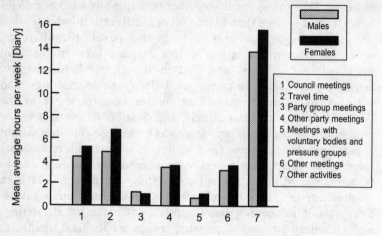

FIGURE 3.2   Councillors' workloads, by gender

Figure 3.3 presents some interesting differences. This looks at workload composition in terms of the major political parties. Labour members attend fewer council and committee meetings (in contrast to findings in the Widdicombe survey), spend more time on travel and very much more time on 'other activities'.

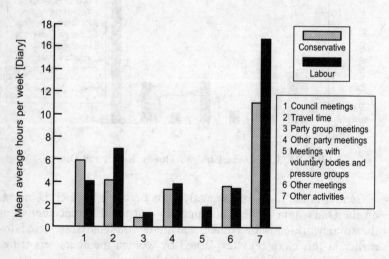

FIGURE 3.3   Councillors' workloads, by party

Council position – that is, whether or not the councillor held an office such as Chair of a committee or major sub-committee – is the subject of Figure 3.4. The most striking difference here is, once again, in terms of 'other activities' with Chairs reporting a figure nearly 50 per cent greater than backbenchers – no doubt reflecting more frequent contacts with officers. Only in category 4 – 'other party meetings' – did backbenchers record a higher figure. With respect to council and committee meetings, we had expected that by virtue of their position Chairs would record a much higher figure than backbenchers. In fact, the difference was much less than we anticipated but was broadly in line with the Widdicombe survey.

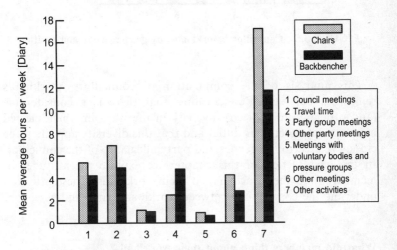

FIGURE 3.4   Councillors' workloads, by council position

Finally, in Figure 3.5 we contrast the two 'extreme' cases – male Conservative backbenchers and female Labour Chairs. Here, the two greatest proportional differences were with respect to 'travel time' and 'other activities' where female Labour Chairs reported spending more than twice the time of that of male Conservative backbenchers. 'Other party meetings' were attended more by the male Conservative backbenchers but they did not report *any* time spent on meetings with voluntary groups and pressure groups.

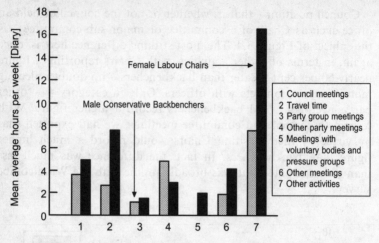

FIGURE 3.5   Councillors' workloads, by gender, party and position

This analysis of the composition of councillors' workloads reinforces our earlier conclusions: that there is a considerable (and officially unreported) diversity in the ways in which elected members interpret their duties and that this diversity appears to be closely related to the gender and party allegiance of the councillor. In the next section of this chapter we explore the attitudes of members (and their partners) to their workloads. These attitudes underline the connections between workload, party and gender.

What did members think about their workloads?

Comments by councillors on their workloads were readily forthcoming. Some stressed the way in which the formal business of the council, scheduled weeks and months in advance, structured their days:

> Your council diary gives you throughout the year the dates and shows you the meetings . . . and the pattern of life shows itself . . . Tuesdays, Thursdays and Saturday mornings are my golf . . . to a large extent one does discipline oneself to it. (Hugh Fordham, Conservative Chair).

I have to attend an executive from 9.30, so my day starts at 9.30 twice a month and it goes on till – with council it usually finishes about 3.30, but by the time you've got hold of an officer . . . time goes on. (Julia Freed, Labour backbencher).

For others, in contrast, it was the irregular and unpredictable nature of their workloads which they emphasised. Not all council meetings, for example, can be anticipated. Sometimes important local issues emerge which generate extra meetings and meetings with pressure groups or town councils. These have to be slotted in at short notice. The following comment from a Conservative backbencher conveys a picture of a somewhat frenetic life:

It's a perfectly random sort of plan. You see the thing that has made this next fortnight very fraught is that we have a Town Plan being put forward which . . . the County Council are discussing, so I'm invited along to the County Council discussions and also we're having extra meetings..and you get this to-ing and fro-ing . . . It's most difficult fitting in every meeting in the middle of what you already have . . . (Herbert Jeffreys, Conservative backbencher).

Casework is likely to be even more unpredictable than meetings. This was the aspect of their work which councillors mentioned most frequently, especially Labour and Liberal members. Some demands made of members included matters which were, strictly speaking, not their responsibility at all – 'They rely on me to sort it out . . . people get very frightened by forms from the DHSS . . .'. Constituents could call at any time:

How do you cope with someone who rings you up and says, 'Look, water is coming through my roof, will you come and see it', and you're in the middle of doing something . . . Do you respond, or do you say, 'Look it's Sunday?' (Janet Baker, Labour Chair).

For others, it was neither committee meetings nor casework which determined their lives but a task often forgotten by members of the public and not usually anticipated by those who seek elected office – the unending flow of paperwork:

I have a desk that looks like a sewer purely and simply because there's a hell of a lot of work to be done. Always got a briefcase full of paper. I'm reading on trains, aircraft that sort of thing. (Robert Paulton, Conservative Chair).

A third of our sample were putting in forty or more hours a week on council and council-related activities. One typical comment here was:

Normally when the thing's going flat out I'm lucky if I get half a day and an evening a week [free] and that includes Sundays. (Margaret Winch, Conservative Chair).

The partner of one of these 'full-time' councillors was well aware of the magnitude of the commitment being made:

The pressures on any county councillor that is trying to do the job properly are murder . . . It's taking forty to forty-five hours a week of her time, and that's a full working week really . . . It can be three or four hours in the morning and go to one of the extraneous bodies in the afternoon . . . and then visit an old people's home . . . and then if you count sometimes two, sometimes three hours that she's sitting reading minutes . . . there's your eight or nine hour day without any trouble at all. (Mr Evans, husband of Labour Chair)

Approximately a fifth of our respondents saw the distinctive character of their constituency as the source of much of the work they had to do. Those county councillors with extensive rural divisions will echo this comment:

I have an enormous rural division which was sheer folly and madness in the reorganisation of boundaries . . . I have thirteen parish councils . . . There is a considerable workload attached to all these parishes . . . they get excited about schools, small schools, highways in particular . . . and all the minutiae of village life . . . . (Leila Hilton, Conservative Chair)

Some respondents, and their partners, remarked on how their workload had increased over the years. Sometimes this was explained in terms of their growing involvement – 'It's like a drug, this politics and council work' – but in other instances it was felt that the demands made on *all* councillors had increased. The barrage of legislation to which we referred in Chapter 1 is reflected in a another comment from Leila Hilton who was a senior member of one county's education committee:

> I think if you look back five, six, seven years . . . it was totally different to now. If you think of the axe that we've had, for example '80, '81; developments with the MSC [Manpower Services Commission]; new exams, total change in a very short space of time . . . This has increased the workload because we spend a lot of time consulting and explaining to people. (Leila Hilton, Conservative Chair).

It is clear from these comments that members and their partners view their workload in very different ways. Some see the cycle of council business as structuring their lives; others stress the unpredictability of the demands made of them. Most emphasised the onerous nature of what they do, but attributed the burden to a variety of sources – the unstoppable flow of paperwork, the nature of their ward, the addictive character of the commitment or the volume of legislation.

How councillors try to cope

On the question of coping with their workload, we had a very large number of comments. Paperwork was uppermost in councillors' minds and it also formed a significant proportion of their workload. Most members chose between two contrasting strategies. The first – which was employed more by women than by men – was selective reading. This was sometimes combined with a scanning or rapid reading approach. Several members remarked that, with experience, they found it much easier to sort out the relevant passages and to discard the rest. Most of those who mentioned selective reading appeared to employ similar criteria: they read thoroughly anything that related to their constituency or to any committee or sub-committee of which they were the Chair or Vice-Chair. Over a period of time, familiarity with and repetition of topics meant that they had to spend less time on detailed reading. On the other hand, those who became leading councillors found they needed to maintain an overall picture of what was going on and that increased their workload again.

The second strategy for dealing with paperwork was to deal with it 'thoroughly'. This approach was favoured disproportionately by men. These councillors insisted that in order to fulfil their council duties properly, they had to go through all the papers supplied for each meeting – not just once but several times.

We are unclear about the reasons for this gender difference. Perhaps women find that their multiple obligations to their families as well as to the council necessarily mean that selective reading is the only practicable way of managing this aspect of their workload. It is possible, also, that women overstate the demands of public office and are then more sharply aware than men of their 'failure' to attain a high standard of performance.

One factor which makes councillors' lives more difficult is the widespread lack of secretarial assistance. In 1982 the Association of Councillors recommended that a full range of services, including secretarial assistance, research and information facilities, photo-copying, help with filing and the provision of stationery should be available when required. In their conclusions they stated firmly:

> Because councillors have survived in an amateur environment for so long is no reason why they should continue to devote scarce energy to the process of survival as distinct from doing an ever increasing job . . . There can be no room for pride in muddling through. (Thomas Report 1982, p. 23)

Only limited progress seems to have been made since then. Whereas in 1980 (the year when the Association of Councillors' survey was conducted) only 33 per cent of authorities reported providing secretarial services to all members, 55 per cent of councils responding to the Widdicombe postal questionnaire claimed that they were doing so (Widdicombe 1986b). Less encouragingly, the report of the Widdicombe interview survey remarked that backbenchers' accounts of the provision of secretarial help were very different from those of chief executives. Perhaps this is not surprising for where two or three secretaries are provided for a full council of 60 or 70 members, it is almost inevitable that most of their time will be taken up by leading members of the council (Widdicombe 1986b, p. 75).

Lack of significant progress in the provision of secretarial facilities was confirmed in a second inquiry carried out by the Association of Councillors. In 1985, 45 per cent of the authorities which were questioned provided secretarial services for all members, an increase of 8 per cent on the 1980 figure. A partial service was available in 64 per cent of authorities in 1980 but by 1985 this figure had dropped to 51 per cent. Where a limited service was available to members, in both 1980 and 1985 the principal beneficiaries were mayors, council leaders and chairs. In 1985, fewer authorities provided secretarial services for opposition leaders than in 1980 (Association of Councillors 1987, p. 50). The Association concluded:

> What does seem clear, from the evidence, is that the level of administrative support available to elected members may be so low as to prevent many from playing a full part in a local democratic system of government. (Association of Councillors 1987, p. 66)

The most that the councillors in our sample could expect was occasional typing or secretarial assistance.

> I find it's dangerous taking [work] into County Hall because the secretary is never available when I am, and it just doesn't get done. One doesn't get the back-up service one should have with the job. (Margaret Winch, Conservative Chair)

In our view, the bulk of the paperwork will remain to be dealt with by the councillor whatever level of secretarial assistance is provided by councils. This is, however, part of a much wider issue of how members adapt to the demands made of them, how they see their role and what facilities should be provided to assist members. We will return to this important question in Chapters 7 and 8.

'. . . something has to be abandoned . . .'

Turning to how members limit their work, we received twice as many comments from women than from men. Limitation took a variety of forms. Some councillors were determined to limit their committee memberships – 'I felt I'd rather know one committee well than three committees and not really understand them.' – but others cut down on meetings of outside bodies such as parish councils and voluntary bodies. For example, a Conservative woman chair commented:

> I've come off a lot of committees that I served on before I became a county councillor, because, you know, if you can't go to the meeting, you shouldn't be a member of committees. That worried me because I couldn't manage the workload . . . .
> (Maureen Porter, Conservative Chair)

In many cases it was clear that members experienced a gradual build-up of commitments followed by some form of 'crisis' (perhaps triggered by domestic or employment problems) when a drastic reappraisal took place. For example:

> I've been trying ever since we moved [house] . . . to make sure we cut down as much as possible on our evening meetings . . . .
> (Carol Stothard, Conservative backbencher)

Equal determination was shown by some councillors to protect their weekends. Many were very reluctant to attend meetings but some (most commonly Labour chairs) commented on their inability to keep their weekends free from interruption. A small number (all Conservatives in one Conservative controlled authority) refused adamantly to take on any work at that time of the week.

> As far as I'm concerned I'm a five day councillor. I feel the weekend's for my wife and family, and if people phone me up on a Sunday or anything like that – I was taught at an early age, 'Never on Sunday'. (Hugh Fordham, Conservative Chair)

For many members, however, Sunday is a time for catching up on the paperwork – preparing for the following week's committees and group meetings. Casework constantly intrudes into the private life of councillors and many are resigned to phone calls interrupting their leisure. But most try to limit those activities that are within their control so as to keep at least Sundays free from too many public commitments. We will explore this aspect further in Chapter 5.

Councillors, therefore, try in a variety of ways – dealing with paperwork, abandoning commitments, protecting leisure time – to balance their public duties and their private obligations to family and employment. For some, however, this 'balance' becomes more difficult to maintain and their lives are pervaded by a sense of pressure, even of crisis, as commitments mount and conflicts between competing demands on time become sharper. We now move on to consider some of the pressures that arise from their council work.

Pressures on councillors: the wider view

We referred earlier to the interview survey of 550 councillors and officers which was conducted for the Widdicombe inquiry. In 85 per cent of the councils which they visited the balance of opinion was that the time required of, or actually being worked by, members had increased in recent years. The interviewers asked members for their explanations of why and in what ways those time demands had increased. Table 3.2 sets out under a series of summary headings the reasons most commonly put forward. These range along a continuum from those reasons which are 'externally imposed' to those which are largely 'self-generated'.

We discussed earlier (see Introduction) some of the possible reasons for the increased demands on councillors' time. Among external pressures are those relating to the increased size of wards. Apart from the abolition of the six metropolitan county councils, the Greater London Council and the Inner London Education Authority there have been very few changes to the external boundaries of local authorities since 1974. In contrast, however, internal ward boundaries have been subject to review and modification. In some cases the number of wards has been reduced significantly. Where this has been accompanied by a reduction in the number of members, those councillors remaining are inevitably

TABLE 3.2   Pressures on councillors

EXTERNALLY IMPOSED	←——————————→	SELF-GENERATED

Structural changes to local government
e.g. larger authorities and larger wards.

   Electoral pressures
   e.g. increasing electoral volatility,
   more hung councils.

      Socio-demographic changes
      e.g. increasing number of old people.

         Economic pressures
         e.g. scarcer resources, unemployment.

            Central government pressures
            e.g. more complicated legislation,
            more central intervention

               Community pressures
               e.g. from local parties and interest
               groups

                  Councillors' own interests
                  e.g. implementing the manifesto,
                  distrust of senior officers.

Adapted from Widdicombe 1986b, p. 63.

required to take over responsibility both for new and possibly unfamiliar areas and for new and almost certainly unfamiliar problems.

Other sources of pressure relate to the changing political composition of councils. Electorally, the emergence of 'hung' or 'balanced' councils has been a remarkable feature of the 1980s. For example, after the district elections in England and Wales in 1987, in almost a third of the non-metropolitan districts no party had a majority of the seats (*Social Trends* 18, 1988, Table 11.12).

The Widdicombe researchers found that councillors and officers were in general agreement that 'hung' councils had led to increased workloads for everyone. Much more time is spent in preparation for meetings, since any party group may be in a position to influence decisions; council and committee meetings are taking longer and have to be more conscientiously attended because they have become genuine arenas for taking decisions; and more decisions are taken to full committee as the Chair's freedom of action has become more limited.

The pressures which the members in the Widdicombe survey mentioned most frequently were those stemming from central government (Widdicombe 1986b, p. 64). Recent legislation, some of which was described in our Introduction, was undoubtedly *felt* by councillors to be responsible for a major increase in members' workloads, and particularly for leading councillors. It was also commonly suggested that the handling of financial contraction was a much more difficult and demanding exercise than the management of expansion.

In contrast, councillors are able to respond more selectively to 'community pressures'. The Widdicombe researchers found that some councillors acknowledged and responded to demands from the local community or ward more vigorously and positively than others. As we will describe in Chapter 7, the members we spoke to responded in a similar way.

Finally, members bring to their council work their own interests and priorities. For example, some are strongly driven by their ideological commitment and wish to bring about major changes in the local authority's relationship with the community. Moreover, many members are no longer content with the formal adoption of their party's manifesto in the event of gaining power. They have increasingly come to see the carrying out of that manifesto's pledges as a major political priority and seek a close involvement with senior officers to ensure that their party's objectives are being pursued. In short, these members see the ways in which a local authority works as just as crucial an issue as what the council does in terms of its powers and services.

Pressures: the personal experience of councillors

The information provided by the Widdicombe interview survey is valuable in that it gives a macroscopic view of how the world of the councillor has become more demanding and the duties more onerous. Such a survey does, however, have certain weaknesses. The information is highly generalised and this makes it difficult to relate the sense of pressure to any particular set of issues, circumstances or types of local authority. Moreover, in spite of talking about 'self-generated' pressures, the authors of the survey attributed the growing pressures almost exclusively to the 'external' public world of elections, legislation and casework. They also assumed that as demands on members' time have increased, so have the pressures. This over-simple 'cause–effect' link is one that we wish to question. We suggest that the time spent on formal council work is only one of several aspects of the pressure which councillors experience.

What constitutes 'pressure' is a debatable question. The point at which a heavy workload shades off into a pressured situation will obviously vary from one individual to another and at different times in any one individual's life. We did not attempt to measure 'pressure' by any formal procedures but allowed members and their partners to respond in whatever way they thought appropriate to the questions we put about council work and its effects on the family and on employment. We were particularly careful to ensure that they were able to express any feelings of being pressured (or not) without any suggestion from us that their activities appeared onerous or difficult in some way. We did not, for example, have a explicit set of questions which were designed to elicit 'pressure' responses. In the event, councillors and partners gave 'pressure' answers at many different points in the interviews. Overall, Labour councillors were most likely to cite pressures and least likely to say confidently that they could cope with them. This party effect was most marked in the case of women who, as we noted earlier in this chapter, tended to have greater workloads.

Conflicts and pressures from within the council

A large number of councillors (two-thirds of our sample) and more than a quarter of partners attributed a sense of pressure (as experienced by themselves or their spouses) to one or more aspects of the councillor role. Women were almost twice as likely as men to cite pressures stemming from this source.

As we have suggested above, the Widdicombe interview survey assumed a simple direct link between the demands on members' time and the pressures they experience. With regard to two aspects of councillors' work – council meetings and casework – we found little evidence to justify this assumption. The number and frequency of council and committee meetings was only a minor concern to the members we interviewed. This is, however, consistent with the figures on the composition of councillors' workloads which we discussed earlier in this chapter and which indicated the relative insignificance of formal meetings in relation to the total workload. Partners, in contrast, were much less resigned to this aspect of their spouse's activities. With some bitterness, one partner said:

> I find the pressure of council meetings a bit of a pain – the quantity of Labour Party consultative meetings . . . he has to go to means that I miss out a lot on social life. You know, it's all very well for him to say, 'Oh, well, you can go out with your own friends.' I say, 'Actually I married *you*, funnily enough!' (Mrs Scott, wife of Labour Chair)

We will be exploring this issue more in Chapter 5.

Councillors did not regard casework as a source of pressure, either, even though it formed a substantial part of their workload. They did not see this as a problem but accepted it willingly and without question. We see this as a further clear indication that there is no simple cause–effect relationship between the demands on members' time and any sense of pressure which they experience.

Judging from their comments, a major source of pressure on councillors (and often indirectly on their partners as well) was a pervasive sense of conflict. The many strains and tensions which frequently arise in the course of a council career cannot be measured simply in terms of the hours spent on a particular activity. Many members felt that particularly contentious issues or policy decisions could lead to increased stress and even when a particular policy commands wide support bringing it to fruition can add significantly to the sense of strain:

> If you talk in terms of pressure, [that issue] has been the greatest thing in my life, because the struggle, the battle, the speeches one

has made. I believe I've addressed every chapel right through the valley, up and down everywhere I could speak, in order to gather support in the early days . . . (Ronald Jones, Labour Chair)

Another councillor remarked that the increasing demand for public participation on contentious issues had made her role far more demanding:

When you get a major issue to decide there are loads of extra meetings . . . and of course you've got to fit it all in, and these days, of course, the public want to take a far larger part in everything so you get pressure groups and hundreds of phone calls all the time. (Rose White, Conservative backbencher)

The greatest sense of pressure seemed to stem from conflict within a committee or party group. This was especially stressful:

The thing that upsets me the most, and I'm being perfectly frank with you on this, is if we have any disagreement within our own ranks, and that really does upset me . . . I'm quite prepared to fight the opposition and it doesn't do anything to me, it doesn't upset me because I feel I'm doing the right thing, but I cannot bear to fight my own members. It's such a waste of time and achieves nothing . . . . (Janet Baker, Labour Chair)

Altogether, a third of the respondents mentioned policy issues and decision-making as resulting in increased pressure. While there were almost equal numbers of men and women, men were more likely to see the issue itself as causing the problem, whereas women were rather more likely to cite conflicting views in the party group as being the source of the stress.

Most councillors identified special responsibilities as leading to increased problems. For example, it was quite common for members to remark on the pressures which came from holding a particular office. Those who became chairs or group leaders could find the work onerous.

I don't think pressures on backbenchers . . . are ever very great. But I think they increase for chairmen of committees and obviously for the Chairman of the County Council. The pressures increase enormously because so many decisions go to the top. I think that's difficult. (Charles Rivendell, Conservative Chair)

A number of leading councillors who had held chairs had found the tensions arising from multiple office-holding too much for them. Here again women predominated and were more likely than men to give up office to relieve the strains on them. Sometimes conflicts arose as a result of office holding on two councils:

> It was difficult when I was doing two councils, until I resigned. That was a difficult time, inasmuch as things were being discussed at county and at [district] and opposite views of things . . . You knew things that the borough didn't know, and then you knew things down here the committees didn't know. I found that hard . . . . (Christine Evans, Labour Chair)

Clearly, conflict generates a sense of pressure both before and after a particular event. Whether it is a rancorous party group or a very heated consultative meeting with community interests – for example, concerning the possible closure of a school – the pressures created can endure and easily intrude into and interact with all that a member does whether council work, employment or family life.

Conflicts and pressures from outside the council

We have suggested that a comprehensive picture of the pressures experienced by councillors (and their partners) must embrace their private worlds as well as the more easily observed aspects of their activities such as meetings, group policy disputes and the offices they hold. Problems with their families and employment were mentioned by approximately one in five of councillors.

Interestingly, most of these comments came from backbenchers. It is possible that those members who take on some additional responsibility – a committee Chair, for example – were more successful in managing the conflicts between their private obligations and council duties. Indeed, it could be that their success in this regard had enabled them to seek or accept additional responsibilities.

We found that women were more likely than men to identify the family as a source of pressure but, as the following quotations illustrate, women emphasised the practical difficulties which arose whereas men expressed feelings of guilt more than any clear determination to remedy the problem.

I suppose in my cycle there is one week when I've got a lot of committee meetings . . . then if you add on to that the outside organisations I'm also involved in, then sometimes I'm out of the house every day of the week. When that happens, that gets a bit frantic because there are always arrangements to make . . . Some things start early, that means I've got to make arrangements pre-school . . . and she's got to be met by someone at twenty past three . . . . (Julia Freed, Labour backbencher)

Being out pretty well every night, I think that's one of the main problems, and being told you put other people before you family, that's one of the biggest problems. (Tim Meeson, Labour backbencher)

It is clear that the family is a significant source of pressure for a substantial minority of councillors and that those who are most affected are women councillors and backbenchers. (We will return to these questions in Chapters 4 and 5.)

Conflicts between the demands of employment and those of the council were a further source of pressure on some councillors. We consider the legal position and particular difficulties of councillors who are in employment in Chapter 6. Here we simply wish to look at employment as a source of pressure upon members. Men were more than twice as likely as women to experience conflict between their employment and their council work. This largely reflects the greater number of men in employment or self-employment (20 men and 8 women). Men saw the demands of paid work as inescapable as women saw the demands of their families.

For a number of years, I worked a night shift, and I was attending meetings during the day, and that's when the pressures were sometimes great, when you're very tired. (Andrew Moore, Labour backbencher)

When I was elected to the council and actually winning control of the county council, we had policies to implement, we had at the same time the government's decision to withdraw money from the county council which meant another 9 per cent on the rates . . . there was a tremendous amount of pressure on attending meetings . . . which created tremendous problems with work – and home may I say . . . . They were very trying times all round. I almost lost my job at work because of the amount of time I was spending in [County Hall]. (Gordon Tranter, Labour backbencher)

The kinds of difficulties reflected in these two quotations can possibly explain the significant fall in recent years in the proportion of councillors in paid employment (60 per cent in 1985 as opposed to 72 per cent in 1976). (Widdicombe 1986c, p. 28). Moreover, in the past the political parties have depended on a substantial 'pool' of non-employed women from which to recruit some of their candidates for local elections. If, as is widely anticipated, this 'pool' contracts as more women go out to work, we feel it is likely both that the political parties will experience greater recruitment difficulties and that councils will not be able to benefit from the same wide variety of experience of employment of their members.

A rather different kind of outside pressure can come from conflict with the media. On one occasion a local newspaper urged readers to telephone their local councillors:

Well we had some abusive calls then, and unfortunately Graham was at a meeting all night so I managed to grab those . . . . (Mrs Lancaster, wife of Labour Chair)

Once your number's out in public, you tend to get aggressive calls . . . The only one that was really unpleasant was in the middle of the night. (Janice Painter, Labour Chair)

Only Labour members and their partners mention media intrusion of this kind. All were in the same authority, and all but one were Chairs – indicating perhaps that they had had to deal with some especially contentious issues, resulting in their widespread unpopularity.

It is clear to us that the pressures experienced by councillors which come from outside the council originate in various conflicts of obligation. Some members found difficulties in managing their family responsibilities. Others experienced difficulties with their paid work. We will look at how they responded to these problems in the following two chapters.

Voluntary retirement as a response to pressure

The most direct response which a member can make when the demands of office become intolerable is either to resign immediately or not to seek re-election. Unfortunately, little is known about why members give up council work. There is little doubt, however, that the turnover of councillors has increased. For instance, as we mentioned in Chapter 2, the number of councillors who have served for 10 years or more is significantly lower today (35 per cent) than it was at the time of the Maud survey in 1964 (48 per cent) and the proportion of members with 21 or more years of service has fallen dramatically (from 10 per cent to 3 per cent) since the middle of the 1970s. The turnover of councillors does not appear to be uniform and is concentrated in the metropolitan and larger shire district authorities and amongst backbenchers and minority group members (Widdicombe 1986b, pp. 47–50).

Clearly a major reason for this increased turnover is that since the reorganisation of local government in the early 1970s there has been a dramatic drop in the proportion of councillors returned unopposed (70 per cent in the 1964 rural district elections as opposed to less than 5 per cent in the English and Welsh district elections in 1988) (Maud Report, Vol. I, p. 93; Rallings and Thrasher 1988, Vol. II, p. ii).

Councillors also retire on grounds of age and health. But it is clear from the Widdicombe interview survey that the considerable commitment required of members was commonly quoted as a cause of voluntary retirement. Younger councillors in the 25–40 age range (particularly in the metropolitan districts, London boroughs and Scottish districts where there has been a marked increase in the last decade) with career prospects and young families, are likely to face major difficulties trying to reconcile the demands of council work with their other obligations (Widdi-combe 1986c, Table 2.4).

These difficulties become intensified where an authority holds daytime meetings and operates on a short committee cycle (four- instead of six-weekly). This can have the effect, as the Widdicombe researchers reported, of minimising the challenge of 'newcomers' to the more elderly, established members of a council. It is clear that the timing, length and frequency of meetings can affect signific-antly the occupational composition of a council (Widdicombe 1986b, p. 53).

Adapting to the demands of office

Those councillors who have no wish to retire voluntarily and who may have long-term personal and political ambitions have to adapt to what they find are the inescapable features of the office: the considerable and diverse workload, the remorseless stream of cases from constituents and the unending flow of papers to scan or to scrutinise. They have to learn to cope as best they can without significant secretarial assistance and be prepared to say 'No!' when the demands on them jeopardise what they believe is the essential core of their work. They have to develop a resilience to the many pressures on them and their families and manage the conflicts which arise from their public duties and private obligations.

Those who intend to stay in office must evolve strategies which provide a more or less stable reconciliation of the conflicting demands they face. As we will illustrate in the following chap-ters, the private world of partner, family and employment is *always* an active ingredient in this process of adaptation together with the more familiar and more observable demands of constituents, party and council colleagues and the issues of the day.

In many hours of interviews, councillors and their partners have shown us a very rich variety of these adaptive strategies. From these, we have tried to identify some recurrent patterns and have developed a threefold categorisation of political styles or roles: politics as a hobby; politics as a vocation; and politics as a job. We will return to these three distinctively different political styles in Chapter 7 after we have examined in detail the private world of the councillor.

PART III
THE PRIVATE WORLD

4   Family Life as Work

I mean I need a good wife, I really do. When I'm out of the house, there's nobody here, nobody to do all of those things. (Ann Harris, Labour Chair)

Introduction

Having looked at councillors' public workload, we now turn our attention to a major innovative aspect of the book: politicians' private lives. In this section of the book, we will be taking account of the findings of both our studies, and setting them within the context of what is known about family life and gender roles in the family in Britain today. We try to answer some of the questions which previous studies have rarely touched on: What are the consequences of political activity for family life? Are partners supportive of their politically active spouses? Do women have a harder time of it than men? And what are the effects on the children?

Our findings show that both male and female activists value enormously the support they get from their partners. The nature and amount of that support tends, however, to vary on gender lines. Men take for granted their wives' practical help, and only rarely put much value on it. Women, in contrast, are often particularly in need of practical help with running the home, and particularly appreciative when it is forthcoming; but even more important in their eyes, is their husbands' stated commitment to the work they are doing. Clearly, the perceptions these women and men had of the help they were giving and getting were conditioned by stereotypical notions of male and female tasks.

Gender roles and family life

Family commitments may affect the extent and nature of an individual's community involvement. Conversely, a heavy public workload – such as is shouldered by many of those described in Chapter 3 – can have considerable implications for other household members. Yet surprisingly, the family commitments of councillors and other political activists have been treated only cursorily, if at all, in previous studies in this area.

In order to explore these issues, we will need to look first at the general nature of family life, with particular reference to white families in Britain. We can see this as having two contrasting aspects. Firstly, there is the work that is generated by family and household living. This is the subject of the present chapter. Secondly, in Chapter 5, we focus on the relaxation and leisure time which individuals spend with other family members. In both cases, experiences are strongly conditioned by age and gender: adults and children, and men and women, have different kinds of duties and responsibilities, and gain different benefits and pleasures from living in family groups.

In looking at the household workload, the sexual division of labour is of particular significance. So, also, are any changes to this division of labour that may have been made as a result of one partner taking on the additional commitments of political life. The notion of 'support' is relevant here. Support can take a number of forms. For example, a partner may take over some of the practical tasks in the home which were originally done by the activist. Other partners may undertake, or help with some of the council member's public duties. (This aspect will be dealt with more fully in Chapter 5.) Other forms of assistance are less obvious, but entail encouragement and emotional support to enable the council member to undertake her or his tasks happily and effectively. All these factors have to be taken into account in looking at the difficulties and the satisfactions of local political activity.

The home as workplace

For many people, regarding the home as a workplace and family life as labour are incongruous notions. 'Work' is conventionally seen as something we are paid to do. This definition rules out cleaning and maintaining our own homes, caring for our children, and all voluntary activities – including, of course, council work itself. More recently, some sociologists have challenged this view, and those concerned with the sociology of work and industry are reluctantly beginning to recognise that the automatic equation of 'work' with 'paid employment' is unacceptable (see for example, Deem and Salaman 1985, Littler 1985). This redefinition of the nature of work is related to the feminist insistence that the boundary between the public and private worlds is not fixed but a reflection of social values, and, like the division of labour in the home, is an essentially political issue.

It is only relatively recently that sociologists have begun to treat the work involved in running one's own home explicitly as a job, like any other (Oakley 1974); one which could provide job satisfaction or the reverse, and result in alienation in the same way as work in a factory or an office could do. Earlier studies have looked at the sexual division of labour (Bott 1971, Gavron 1966, Rapoport and Rapoport 1971, Blood and Wolfe 1965), and established conclusively – to no-one's surprise – that women not only do considerably more housework than men, but they typically spend the equivalent of a full-time working week on it (in excess of forty hours) whether or not they are also in full-time paid employment outside the home.

Men's work in the home has been accorded much less attention. Many researchers interviewed women only (Oakley 1974, Gavron 1966, Blood and Wolfe 1965), either because they chose to focus on women's experiences, or because women were generally more easily available and willing to talk about such issues. Even when both men and women were interviewed, and notwithstanding the eagerness of some researchers to include 'typically male' tasks in their checklists, or to regard male 'help' once or twice a week as an indication of almost complete 'symmetry' (Willmott and Young 1975, Newson and Newson 1963, 1970) women's generally higher household workload is incontrovertible. A recent study of newly-married couples showed that even when partners aimed to share tasks equitably, men still retained the prerogative to choose *which* chores they do (Mansfield and Collard 1988); and it was the wife rather than the husband who cut down her working hours outside the home if she found difficulties in coping with 'her' household responsibilities. Other studies have shown repeatedly that men tend to choose occasional tasks (painting the house, mowing the lawn), those involving major spending decisions (choosing furniture, booking a holiday) and those which they enjoy (bathing the children, or playing cricket or Monopoly with them).

While none of these tasks has the unremitting constancy of most day-to-day housework and childcare, nevertheless they play an important part in family life. Male political activists – like other men with heavy workloads outside the home – may often find it a struggle to carry on doing all these things, but their difficulties and stresses tend to be ignored. Only one study, to our knowledge, has pointed out that men might also experience conflict in reconciling their family responsibilities with their political ambitions (Sapiro 1982). Men, however (at least on this evidence), tend to 'resolve' this conflict by withdrawing from family life to a large degree; rather than delaying their entry into politics, or working out coping strategies, as women usually do. This clearly has implications for their partners and other family members, but once again, the tendency of social scientists to focus *either* on the public world *or* on the private one has obscured this relationship.

Private and public worlds

The first and largest body of studies to link the public and private worlds were those which looked at 'women's two roles' of paid work and home. Early studies were concerned with potential problems: for example, did the children suffer? and what strategies did the women employ in order to cope with their 'dual burden'? (Jephcott *et al.* 1962, Myrdal and Klein 1956, Klein 1965). Often there was the implication that women who 'chose' to work outside the home were indulging themselves, and therefore had to cope with the consequences themselves. Later studies, inspired in part by the feminist movement which developed from the late 1960s onwards, endorsed the rights of both women and men to play a full part in all aspects of life. They also recognised, however, that in practice, most women's choices were very limited, and working class women, at any rate, were forced to work in unfulfilling jobs for most of their lives (Pollert 1981, Westwood 1984, Cavendish 1982).

In this literature, childcare – rather than housework or other family responsibilities – has been regarded as the major obstacle to women's full involvement in public life. In contrast, a more interesting and radical viewpoint – which has implications also for the study of men – is that of Janet Finch. In her pathbreaking study, *Married to the Job* (1983), Finch insists that it is not simply child-rearing but marriage itself that adds disproportionately to women's workload, while easing that of men. From her examination of a wide variety of research, Finch concludes that there is a two-way relationship between a wife and her husband's work. Firstly, his job imposes structures on her life, which constrain her choices and limit (to a greater or lesser extent) her autonomy. Secondly, wives contribute both directly and indirectly to the work that men do. Finch, and later Hilary Callan, refer to this process as 'incorporation' (Callan and Ardener 1984). As a result, not only are women disadvantaged by their struggle to fulfil the various demands on their time, but men can expect, and get, both practical and emotional support from their spouses in undertaking their own workload. This is often of great benefit – and sometimes indispensable – in ensuring men's occupational advancement. The saying that there is a woman behind every successful man is a popular acknowledgement of a situation, which has also been referred to as a 'two-person career' (Papanek 1973; see also Fowlkes 1980, Mortimer *et al.* 1978). This unreciprocal 'incorporation' of women into men's work makes it especially difficult for women to have an independent career of their own – whether that is in the world of employment, or in local or national politics.

While research into 'women's two roles' in employment and the home has been well-established for a number of years, the family commitments of councillors and other political activists is a subject that, until recently, has been treated only cursorily, if at all. In the 1950s and 1960s, political scientists such as Maurice Duverger (1955) and Robert Lane (1959) regarded women's reliance on their husbands' political judgement as 'natural' and their political inactivity as desirable – since even to go out to vote would take time and attention away from their children 'to whom it rightfully belongs' (Lane 1959, p. 355). With the beginning of the 1970s, however, researchers were taking a more critical stance, and women's unequal burden began to be seen as problematic, in preventing their full participation in the 'public' worlds of paid employment and political activity. It is now becoming commonplace to point to the relationship between women's home responsibilities (particularly child-care) and their under-representation in the political sphere (Lynn and Flora 1973, Jennings and Niemi 1981, Hills 1980). A number of writers have referred to 'life style constraints' (Hills 1980, 1982) or 'role conflict' (Sapiro 1982) which are seen as creating particular problems for female politicians at both a local and a national level. To our knowledge, there have been no detailed studies of how successful women politicians manage the two sides of their lives.

Family pressures may also be experienced by male council members and their families (Sapiro 1982) albeit in different ways. As we suggested earlier, these pressures may be responsible for the high turnover of council members which has caused some concern to the Widdicombe Committee (1986b, pp. 47–55). At the level of American state legislatures, Diane Blair and Ann Henry (1981) suggest that family considerations may be an important factor in explaining the dropout rate. (A relatively high proportion of the councillors we interviewed in our studies have stood down in the three years since we talked to them.) The study of newly-elected councillors by Eddison, Fudge, Murie and Ring (Eddison *et al.* 1978, Fudge *et al.* 1979) points out that councillors' families often put up with considerable inconvenience, and sometimes made a contribution to the overall workload; they find no evidence, however, of a rearrangement of household tasks to allow women council members more easily to accommodate council work. Their study confirms that the passing comments of Rees and Smith (1964, p. 61) are still relevant: whereas women who aspire to a council position need to ensure not only that they can cope with the extra work, but that their husbands will give them *active* encouragement before they start, men are more likely both to assume their wives' acquiescence – and to get it.

Throughout our study, we have emphasised that men, as well as women, have private lives, just as women (as well as men) have public ones. We believed, however, that the interrelationships between these two spheres could be different for men and women, and that women activists might find some aspects of these two worlds somewhat more difficult to reconcile. And so it proved to be.

Support between married couples

As we have seen, research into how married couples divide practical tasks between them is well-established. We have suggested, however, that the notion of 'support' is rather wider than the simple undertaking of tasks. In everyday understanding, 'supportiveness' includes encouragement, acceptance, and emotional support of all kinds. The willingness to listen, to give advice, to comfort and to praise are important attributes in any partnership. Research into 'ordinary' marriages is quite limited, however; and most of the studies tend to concentrate on 'who does what?' rather than mutual support in the widest sense (Stephen Edgell 1980, Pahl and Pahl 1971), and we know very little about the quality or quantity of companionship, conversation and emotional support that spouses provide for each other.

An exception is the recent study of 65 newly-married couples (Mansfield and Collard 1988). They show that while both young men and young women now define marriage in terms of a personal relationship rather than an economic unit, there are important differences in their need to communicate and confide in each other. Many men saw no reason for *any* confidante, unless the other person was able to give advice or practical support. They therefore only talked to their wives about their problems at work if they believed the women had a special expertise in the issues under discussion. Women, on the other hand, valued the chance to 'air their feelings' with their spouse – and felt hurt when their husbands appeared neither to want to listen to them, nor had the same need for self-disclosure themselves.

This picture coincides with the widely-held view that women, in contrast to men, put the greatest value on companionship and communication in their relationships and has been supported by the findings of socio-psychological research. Kay Deaux (1976) summarises the evidence from a number of studies which emphasise women's greater social responsiveness and willingness to disclose personal information. A more recent but limited study appears to come to similar conclusions (Wheeler, Reiss and Nezlak 1983). Jessie Bernard's work on 'his' and 'her' marriage also indicates that male and female expectations and satisfactions are not always compatible (Bernard 1972).

This is confirmed in a rather different way by research undertaken by Janet Askham into ordinary marriages (Askham 1984). She attempted to test empirically Berger and Kellner's assertion (Berger and Kellner 1964) that marriage is an identity-building relationship in which an individual's identity is validated by her or his regular interaction with one 'significant other', the marriage partner. Askham suggested, however, that the social rules surrounding marriage would tend to inhibit individual development and autonomy, and that this has to be offset against the satisfaction resulting from the stability of having a regular relationship with one significant person. In practice, in marriages which are more or less satisfactory for both partners, a balance has been achieved between the identity-building and stability-building functions of marriage. These potential conflicts between identity and stability may be less easily resolved, however, for married women than for their male counterparts.

To summarise, it seems that men and women may have rather different kinds of needs in their intimate relationships. These differences will not only condition the satisfactions and frustrations they experience in their marriages but are likely to affect the ease with which women and men can combine public office with family life.

Political activists and partners' support

It was in the light of accumulated knowledge regarding the gender division of labour that we looked at the home workload of both male and female councillors and party activists, and that of their partners as well. (The majority of our respondents were married. None – to our knowledge – was living in a homosexual partnership, so we were unable to look at the consequences of political activism on same-sex couples.)

We anticipated that most of the women we talked to would have more to do in the house than men. Also, given our findings regarding the high council-workload of many council members – particularly that of Liberal and Labour women – we felt that their public responsibilities might have a greater impact on women activists. We were interested in whether a politically active individual had to give up doing certain tasks which previously she or he had always undertaken; and whether the partner was in consequence faced with extra tasks in the home. Undertaking this additional workload is one way in which an individual can give practical support to a politically active partner. First of all, however, we will look at the forms of support which are less obvious, but are nonetheless valued by those on the receiving end, such as listening, encouraging, debating alternative courses of action, and proffering affection, relaxation, or stimulation, as circumstances dictate.

It is not surprising, given previous findings regarding the expected roles of husbands and wives, that the concept of 'partner support' means different things according to whether the partner in question is male or female. This did not just apply to practical tasks. In our discussions with both male and female councillors and activists it was clear that the support of their spouse was crucial in their continuing involvement in local politics. 'Without that', said one councillor to us, 'there would be nothing left. We would just go our separate ways.' On the surface, too, both husbands and wives seemed equally happy to provide that support. But when we looked more closely at the nature of the support which was offered and accepted, we found some interesting differences between men and women.

Someone to talk to

Most women appreciated emotional support more than practical help. Women were particularly likely to recognise the value both to themselves and their spouses, of having 'someone to talk to'.

> It is nice to have somebody to let off steam and to unload all your troubles to when things have gone the wrong way. . . . If you've got someone to talk things over with, you get them in proportion better. (Marian Gaines, Liberal councillor)

Those who valued having someone to talk to were not necessarily worried whether or not this evoked a response from the partner. However, a number of partners did give advice, or put forward their opinions on the issues discussed. While men did not seem to have the same wish that women had to discuss all the happenings of the day with their partners – and correspondingly did not see the need to supply a listening ear either – they were rather more ready to appreciate the value of good advice, whether they were giving it to their anxious partners, or asking for it. This ties in with Mansfield and Collard's findings, to which we referred in the previous section (Mansfield and Collard 1988, pp. 174–5).

'Just being there'

The partner's needs – for such things as companionship, emotional reassurance and material help – also varied according to gender. At the very least, husbands liked their wives to be at home when they were there, and to provide the kind of peaceful and smoothly running environment that most men take for granted. One man was very bitter that he was unable to collapse in front of the television with a drink after work because his wife would often still be out and he had to start preparing a meal for the children.

> The problem has often been that the house is just not managed, there is no management of the house *at all*, you know, the shopping is done at extraordinary times, it's not consistent, the ironing is seldom done, the kids have to be met from school, the tea and the meals have to be prepared, and it's just not happening . . . . I cannot stand chaos, I like to have things in a reasonably orderly manner . . . One has got to work in with what the requirements of a civilised way of life require. (Mr Prince, husband of Liberal councillor)

Another man, who ostensibly played a large part in running the household, nonetheless became irritated when he started to cook a meal and his wife had not yet had time to do the shopping. Another husband said he generally worked late because he saw no point in returning to an empty house. His wife on the other hand reacted by taking on more meetings in the mistaken belief that since he was working he would not miss her. Male irritation at domestic disruption sometimes took the form of passive or even active resistance: one man, for example, fed up with his wife's council papers filling the shelves in the kitchen, dumped the whole lot in a nearby skip while she was on holiday. Another man felt that his wife's frequent absences from home were adequate justification for his own adultery.

In Askham's terms, therefore, women were expected to provide the necessary stability to the households, even if this was at the expense of developing their own identity (Askham 1984). Men, on the other hand, felt free to follow their own interests, confident in the knowledge that that their wives would, as a matter of course, cope with the extra household workload and inconvenience consequent on their public role. The wives occasionally complained – particularly about erratic meal times – but on the whole, they adapted to it:

> I don't know what time he's coming home. Sometimes he'll phone me and it looks like it's going on late, so we don't always – well, we hardly ever do plan that we'll have an evening meal at a certain time . . . . Quite often, I'll get on and eat with Harriet, and whenever he comes in, he'll take pot luck. (Mrs French, wife of Liberal councillor)

Some male councillors did recognise that their own frenetic lifestyle imposed an extra burden on their wives – but they still expected them to fulfil it uncomplainingly.

Practical support

Wives were less concerned with their husbands' simple physical presence, and they certainly did not expect their homes to be run for them. They were, however, very appreciative of the small practical ways in which their husbands helped them: cooking meals, washing up, answering the telephone, and babysitting were all valued. In eleven of the households in which the woman was a councillor, either husband or wife or both acknowledged that the man played a greater role in running the home than he would have done had his wife not been active politically.

> Generally sort of housekeeping you know, I mean washing up or vacuuming or putting the washing in. In small ways sort of trying to make the workload easier for her. Not expecting her to

come home and actually have a job, do the council work and also have the housekeeping, you know the actual household chores. Trying to lighten the burden . . . so that she didn't have to do everything the same as she did before she got on. (Mr Lyall, retired husband of Labour backbencher)

In every family in which we were told that the husband had taken on extra chores, the wife was already a councillor. In contrast, none of the politically active women in our recruitment study mentioned that her husband had taken on extra work in the house. On this evidence, it appears that it is only when elected to the council that the enormity of the workload becomes evident; and therefore it is only in the face of the extra workload of public office that the men respond by shouldering a significant proportion of the household chores. Moreover, many of the councillors who had participatory partners felt they were 'lucky' because their husbands were 'good' to them in this way. They believed they had to demonstrate their gratitude frequently, or their husbands would feel their efforts were not appreciated. Even 'allowing' them to carry on with their political activities was valued.

I'm one of those fortunate women who has never had any problem about women's role in life, and my husband has been happy for me to do quite a number of things. (Jill Finch, Conservative backbencher)

Only occasionally and indirectly did women recognise that supportive though their husbands might be, they were *not* getting the same back-up as any man would take for granted. 'I need a good wife – I really do' said one Labour woman, who had recently become Chair of a major committee; whereas Mrs Finch, who is quoted above, went on to say that her husband's acquiescence lasted as long as she kept the home going as well, so 'I've always thought you do two jobs'. Although these women recognised that their husbands were not providing the kind of practical support that almost any *wife* would give, nonetheless, they did not question the inevitability of this situation. Only a 'wife' – who is by definition female – could be relied upon to run the home and be there when she was needed.

Coping with childcare

Conventionally, most of the work of childcare is regarded as women's responsibility. A large number of studies have looked at women's childcare duties (Gavron 1966, Ginsberg 1976, Boulton 1983) and the way in which they can impinge on and interrupt their employment (Yeandle 1984, Fonda and Moss 1976). In the absence of nursery provision, part-time work, flexible hours, job-sharing and special shifts all help women to combine more easily their responsibilities to their families and their paid work. Certain sections of industry and commerce, which are traditionally dependent on female labour, have in recent years made a few concessions, such as introducing special shift-working patterns, and encouraging job-sharing at relatively senior levels. Some local authorities run after-school and holiday playschemes for school-age children, employers occasionally run crèches and workplace nurseries (on which the tax has recently been removed). The majority of employed mothers, however, still use informal care (from relatives and friends) or pay childminders to look after their children during working hours (Jephcott *et al.* 1962, Clarke and Stewart 1982, Bryant *et al.* 1980, Yeandle 1984).

Apart from informal arrangements, these strategies are less effective for women wishing to take up council work. The hours of work may be less than for a full-time paid job, but the commitments are often inflexible: council members must attend when meetings are scheduled, and this is likely to be to the convenience of the majority of male members and officers rather than to women with family responsibilities. Very few councils run crèches, and in fact the county solicitor in one of the authorities in our study suggested that public money may not be used for this purpose. The timing of council meetings – which often run over from late afternoon into the evening – again makes this a less-than-ideal option. (More than half of all council meetings start between 3 and 6 p.m., which are particularly difficult hours for those who have the care of small children. See Widdicombe 1986c, p. 155.) After-school and holiday playschemes, because of their short supply, are often reserved for employed women, single parents, and those perceived to be in greatest need. And childminders though underpaid for the highly responsible work they do, are nonetheless usually too expensive for councillors to pay out of their attendance allowances. Finally, and notwithstanding the potential for party members to take on informally many of the extra chores of their elected representatives, *formal* job-sharing is not, within the current legal definitions, a viable option for intending council recruits.

In spite of these drawbacks, women with children seemed as likely to take on council responsibilities as men in the same situation. A third of the councillors in our first study and more than half the women in our recruitment study had children of school age or below at the time we interviewed them, and a further 21 councillors had children of this age when first elected to the council. Child-care is, in consequence, a potential issue for many engaged in public life, though most of the men we interviewed had partners who would take on the major responsibility for seeing children were looked after.

> **Interviewer**: Who normally does the minding when they're not at school?
> **Councillor**: Tessa, totally. I mean she will see it as her role, totally wrongly, I bitterly regret that we've got ourselves into the position we have, but she will now automatically make sure that she comes rushing home from work to be here for the kids, and it's more or less now taken for granted that I will roll up when I'm able to . . . . (Nicholas French, Liberal councillor; wife with full-time job)

> It's fair to say she has the major responsibility here, so that really is pressure for her, and I think it's a pressure that women councillors tend to be under more than men. (Mr Freed, husband of Labour backbencher)

The issue of childcare was therefore only salient to women and to a small minority of men who were also the prime child-carers in their households.

There seemed to be a tendency for Labour and Liberal women to consider entering the council at a younger age than Conservative women. This meant that their children were younger (primary school age and below) and therefore, they more frequently faced the problem of providing adequate child-care. These women tended to have taken a break from employment in order to care for their children, but regarded the council as an interesting, socially useful substitute for full-time paid work. Conservative women, on the other hand, were more likely to stand for the council after their children had reached secondary school age, when they could perhaps be regarded as 'old enough' to fend for themselves for short periods.

The commonest way for councillors to manage both their childcare and their council commitments was to get someone else to fill in for them at home. As we have seen, most male councillors do this automatically, the preferred person being the partner. Female councillors call on partners also, but usually only for evening babysitting.

> I've got a Labour Party meeting tonight and they're going to follow it up with some sort of social . . . . So I asked Mike, that's my ex-husband – and he said Thursday was out because he had something to do . . . . [But] very often he'll say to me, 'Have you got any meetings this week?', meaning evenings . . . . It doesn't always work out very well, but we are both willing to do this. (Susan Tyler, Labour backbencher)

> My husband is home in the school holidays fortunately and that is really the only way I've managed, could manage personally, because my husband teaches . . . . That's an important point. (Ann Harris, Labour Chair)

It appeared that few of the people we spoke to were very concerned that their political work will affect their children. Both men and women said much less about their children than they had about their partners, and some men said virtually nothing. Where councillors did raise worries or problems, these mostly related to their lack of time to do all they might wish with their children, or as a family. A few candidates also felt the same way, but mostly, at this stage in their political careers, they were managing to keep time aside to give to their children.

Women in fact might have been more adept than men in reserving time for their family life. For example, one very heavily committed Labour Chair described how one morning she allowed herself to be half an hour late for an important meeting because her young son had woken in a bad mood, indicating a need to sort out the source of conflict then and there. Another woman felt that 'anyone could go to a meeting' but that 'my grandchildren are particular to me'. A typical comment was the following:

> Over anything really big, I made it my business to be available then. Certainly over routine things, like making sure they had plenty of clean clothes and had proper meals at proper times, I wasn't particularly good, but I think when it came to anything of real import to them, I tried to be around. (Adrienne Lyons, Labour Chair)

Men, on the other hand, often appeared to believe that if their wives were around, their children did not really need them quite so much, or that they could make up for their frequent absences by giving 'quality time' when they were available.

> I've always tried to say to myself that it's not necessarily the quantity of time you spend with your children, it's the quality I've tried to give. And the time I've spent with my children, I've tried to make as full as possible for them, so I don't think they've missed out a lot. (Gordon Tranter, Labour backbencher)

Alternatively, they relied on their wives to fill in for them, and the wives were usually prepared to take over this responsibility. One Conservative wife, for example, said, 'I made up for it [by doing a lot with my children] when my husband didn't get as much time [to spend with them] as most fathers.'

Taken together, we feel this evidence suggests that men and women have different priorities when balancing the demands of their public and private lives. It appears that women, whatever other concerns they may have, always try to put their children first and ensure that they do not suffer unduly. Council work only appears to obtrude on their family lives when this cannot be avoided – when they have an especially high workload as a result of their leadership position. Men, on the other hand, do not place the same priority on their children. They may regret the time they spend apart from them, but – perhaps because they regard them first and foremost as their wives' responsibility – they do not appear to make special efforts to minimise their absences. The effects of their lack of time or clashing commitments can therefore be experienced across the board, whatever their party or council position.

In spite of obvious problems, many political activists believed that, on balance, their children gained from their parents' public involvement. We will look at this aspect of family life and the related issue of shared time for family leisure in the next chapter.

The 'political household'

From all that we have said so far, it is clear that the councillors and political activists who will have the greatest workload will be the younger married women councillors, with children to care for. This is particularly true of Labour or Liberal Party members who, as we have shown, have the heaviest council workload, too. Some of these women also had paid employment in addition to their various voluntary and political commitments.

One way in which women like this have managed the conflicting demands on their time was to belong to what we have termed a 'political household'. This concept needs some explanation, since in normal usage, all or most of the families we have studied would be regarded as highly politicised. We are using this term in the somewhat specialised sense of a couple who are both politically committed and who support each other's activities for *ideological* (as well as personal) reasons.

Where such a couple has young children, there may be a conscious choice between them as to which is to be the 'public' political representative, and which – at least for a time – is to take more of a back-seat. (The minority of 'intenders' often come from such households.) Both husband and wife will share the same political goals; and the supporting partner (who in our study was invariably the male) will justify his exceptional involvement in household chores on ideological grounds.

An example of one such household was the Painter family. Mrs Painter and her husband are both Labour party activists. Mr Painter is an active trade unionist and Mrs Painter has been active in the women's sections and women's council of the party. Both of them have held office at both ward and constituency level in the party. For Mrs Painter, becoming a councillor was a natural progression from her other activities.

The Painters have two young children, and share childcare with their other commitments. Mr Painter works shifts as a maintenance engineer, and Mrs Painter has no paid employment at present. When neither of them is available, they pay a childminder. Neither of them has much leisure time, nor – because of Mr Painter's shift pattern, do they have normal 'weekends', but they take it for granted as an unintended consequence of the choices they have jointly chosen to make. Both of them are conscious, of the need to *plan* time very carefully, rather than doing things casually as it occurs to them to do them. Their social life is almost completely tied up with the Labour Party.

Mr Painter sees his political activities and interests as complementary to those of his wife. Politics is the main interest of both of them, and political discussion is a constant part of their interaction together, so that, as Mrs Painter says, it is impossible to separate out the 'political' parts of the day from the non-political. This shared commitment makes possible the inconvenience and limitations that council work imposes on this family. The extra problems consequent on being a mother of young children are therefore manageable.

Among recruits, the Stanley family seemed to us to represent a political household in embryo. Again, both were Labour activists and Mr Stanley also undertook a great deal of trade union work. Neither was employed at present, but because Mrs Stanley was potentially able to earn considerably more than her husband, she was intending to look for a full-time job in the near future. In the meantime, both of them spent most of their time on their respective political activities. Because there was very little money for babysitters, they took it in turns to go to evening meetings, and to take on daytime commitments while the other partner cared for their two pre-school daughters. As with the Painters, they regarded their activities as complementary to each other, and would, for example, decide jointly which activities were of sufficient importance for each of them to support, and which could be forgone, at least on this occasion. Although neither had any immediate intention of standing for the local council, they recognised that this would be a possibility. The decision would in any case be a joint one, and the other partner would be prepared to provide all necessary support.

In both households, shared ideological commitment enabled a couple to accommodate a very high joint workload without this resulting in undue strain on the relationship. The level of practical support offered by the husbands was unusual, when compared to that normally given by men; however, it was still considerably less than that given by most of the wives in our sample. Those women whose comments demonstrated resigned acquiesence or bitterness, nevertheless unquestioningly took on major responsibility for the care of their children and the running of their homes, under conditions often made more difficult by their husbands' political involvement. Their behaviour was not, however, recognised by their husbands or themselves as anything out of the ordinary, because they were merely fulfilling the accepted role as 'housewife'; whereas the men who took on these tasks were stepping outside the masculine social norm.

None of the 'political households' in our sample was Conservative. This may have been because few Conservative women (and no Conservative Chairs) had children under 15 at home; whereas there were several Labour and Liberal women councillors in this situation. On the other hand, it could also be related to the nature of the Conservative Party and its recruitment processes – which put relatively little emphasis on ideological commitment or long-term party involvement.

Were the husbands, in these political households, incorporated into their wives' councillor roles, on the Finch and Callan model presented earlier? (Finch 1983, Callan and Ardener 1984). We cannot fully answer this question until we have considered the data on leisure time and intrusions into family life (see the next chapter). We would, however, suggest that the concern – that all women councillors shared – to put their children's interests first, and not to disrupt family routines any more than was essential is in complete contrast to the way in which some men allow their work routines and the demands of their jobs to impinge on family life. Rather than allowing their council workload to structure the household day, women tried as far as possible to fit their public commitments *around* their family responsibilities. Moreover, when their husbands took on additional chores as a direct result of their council work, the women did not take this for granted, but were generally eager to express their gratitude. We will return to this issue in the following chapter.

Conclusion

In this chapter, we have looked briefly at some of the work involved in building a home and caring for children, and have described some of the ways in which political activism can affect an individual's ability to carry out responsibilities in this area. Over the past twenty years, a number of studies have demonstrated that women consistently fulfil more of the total household workload than men, and that the tasks for which they are normally responsible require daily commitment and are less flexible than many of the tasks men undertake. This presents problems for women who wish to have a high involvement in the public world – whether that is in a paid job or as a council member.

Women we spoke to coped with these added difficulties in different ways. Some had partners who took on a greater proportion of the household workload than they normally would have done. Others asked friends or other family members to fill in for them (especially in regard to childcare), or they paid a helper to do some of the household work. Some 'coped' by cutting down on the work they regarded as necessary to family life – sometimes to the irritation or annoyance of other family members.

Men who became councillors disrupted the household in different ways. Often their wives' workload was increased because meals had to be delayed or reheated, and children were compensated for their father's absences by having more attention from their mother. Although some wives complained about the situation, they nonetheless provided unquestioning practical help to enable their husbands to fulfil their public duties without worrying what was going on at home – a luxury few women experienced. Even the most supportive husbands who shared their wives' ideological commitment, and were prepared to further their political involvement, nonetheless failed to provide as much help in practical terms.

Other kinds of support were, however, equally valued. Almost all councillors and most of the women who were standing for election, said that having a partner who believed in what they were doing was an essential prerequisite to political involvement. Many women went further, and emphasised the value of having someone to talk to about what they were doing – whether or not any active response (such as advice) was forthcoming. The wives of male councillors also felt that in listening to their husbands they were providing a valuable service; the men, however, didn't appear to recognise this. Nevertheless it may be that men were gaining something from this even if they did not acknowledge it. This may be the reason wives who undertook all the practical tasks but complained or were unhappy about the extent of their husbands' political involvement did *not* receive much appreciation for their efforts: their husbands felt the lack of wholehearted support, though they were unable to identify the source of their dissatisfaction.

Ideally, then, intending councillors should gain their partners' practical *and* emotional support before embarking on their political careers. One without the other may initially seem to be sufficient; but dissatisfaction is likely to grow, leading either to problems in fulfilling public duties, or difficulties and disappointments in the marital relationship.

5 Family Life, Social Life, and Leisure

I just think what would be nice is not to feel the pressure sometimes, to feel more relaxed and be able to go out and do something with the children instead of feeling that I've got this and that to do . . . . I don't think they're deprived, but it's not quite a normal family life. (Carla Perkins, Labour candidate)

Introduction

Having looked at the work that is involved in family life, we now move on to a consideration of leisure and social relationships. We will be arguing, using illustrative data from our two studies, that 'leisure' is a very equivocal concept. Political activism, when undertaken as a voluntary activity, may in some respects be seen as a 'leisure interest', but only a minority of councillors and other political activists saw it in that way. More commonly, our respondents regarded the time-commitment as a necessary but unfortunate interference to their leisure, and to family leisure activities in particular.

Not all leisure takes place within a family context. Some leisure activities – for example, stamp collecting or jogging – are normally undertaken alone. Other leisure activities are, however, social occasions too, frequently involving other family members, friends and acquaintances. It is customary for married couples, in particular, to go out together and socialise together with other such couples. In either case, change in the time available for leisure or in the activities undertaken is likely to have an impact on other family members.

We will be considering three related questions. What effects does active community involvement have on social relationships? Does political activism and in particular council membership generate a distinct social life of its own? And what is the impact on the leisure activities of other family members?

What is leisure?

To some people, the difference between work and leisure might seem so obvious as to require very little reflection or analysis. An eight hour shift on an assembly line, or typing in an office can only be described as 'work'; whereas a weekend outing to the seaside, or an evening in front of the television or sitting in a pub are usually regarded, unquestioningly, as 'leisure'. This was the customary starting-point for many sociologists who contrasted leisure and paid work (in particular, Stanley Parker's work, 1972 and 1983). Leisure was defined negatively as that part of the day or week which was *not* taken up either in employment (or travelling to work) or in 'self-maintaining' activities such as sleeping and eating. This definition is not, however, very suitable for those – like councillors – who have extensive voluntary commitments, or whose day-to-day work is unpaid.

Others have proposed alternative definitions, focusing on the nature of the activity, the time it is carried out, or the extent to which it is freely chosen and enjoyable for the participants. All these definitions are open to criticism, however. Foremost among the critics have been feminists, who have pointed out that housework, childcare and related activities (as well as gardening, decorating and so on) are either completely ignored or occupy equivocal positions in these male-centred approaches (Deem 1986, Wimbush and Talbot 1988); so, too, is the work which some people – whether as professionals, executives, home-workers or the self-employed – bring home to do after their normal working hours; and, in such definitions, the unemployed, students, and the retired apparently lead a life of unrelieved leisure.

Some more recent studies have developed this argument further and have shown how women are often responsible for providing leisure for men and children (Griffin *et al.* 1982). Family celebrations, for example, are typically organised by women; weekends, bank holidays and Christmas are often occasions when women – whether or not they are also engaged in paid work – experience a very heavy unpaid workload; and self-catering holidays may merely move the workplace from home to a new location. Women, perhaps more frequently than men, engage in two or more activities at once; for example, taking the children swimming while swimming themselves, or knitting while watching TV. This is not to deny that they often enjoy these social and leisure activities, in spite of working at the same time, and in preparation for them.

The same kinds of problems arise when looking at local politicians, whether male or female. Voluntary political work, at council level or within the community, is not normally defined as a 'job'; there is no regular salary, no sick pay, no pension, no redundancy money (as there is for MPs). Unlike most jobs, the timing of much political work is unpredictable and often occurs at 'unsocial' hours. Councillors, in particular (like women), spend much of their free time providing for others' needs, and this includes the provision, funding and maintenance of various facilities for leisure in their areas.

Again, for councillors, as for women generally, the boundaries between work and leisure are not clearly defined. Attending a formal reception, going for a drive to see a site for which a planning application is pending, or walking the dog along a different footpath each day to ensure that all are free of obstruction are examples of the kinds of 'leisure' activities many councillors engage in, and which they – and their families – find more or less enjoyable. On the other hand, when a call from a constituent interrupts Sunday lunch or a relaxing evening in front of TV, the reaction of the councillor and his or her partner may be very similar to those of a parent when a trip to the park or the swimming bath is partially spoilt by a child falling off the slide or starting a fight with a sibling.

'Leisure? – What leisure?'

Many of the councillors and other political activists we talked to were well aware of these ambiguities. We asked everyone, 'What do *you* mean by leisure?' and received a wide variety of replies. Some responded by listing various activities they enjoyed – 'Going out for a drink', 'Gardening', 'Watching TV'. Others defined it in terms of residual time – that which remained after family and political responsibilities and paid work commitments had been fulfilled. A few characterised leisure by its functions – 'It relieves pressure', 'It allows me to relax'. Some demarcated specific periods of time, such as Sundays or holidays, as leisure time; others found it impossible to draw any boundaries; and a sizeable minority of councillors – all of whom were men – said their council work constituted their leisure.

A further group of councillors seemed to share our difficulty in defining 'leisure': they responded noncommittally or with laughter when asked what 'leisure' meant to them. In most cases, this was because they found it difficult to think of any recent leisure activities at all. Shortage of free time was one of the most frequently remarked consequences of an active political life. More than a third of the principle respondents we talked to (councillors, candidates and other activists), said that their social life and leisure activities were to some extent (and sometimes considerably) restricted by their community activism.

I think the thing that has suffered more than anything else, I used to do a lot of oil painting, and I don't do any of that now. I haven't got any time. Possibly my family don't see much of me . . . It probably means I don't get to sit down a lot. (Gina Light, Alliance candidate and parish councillor)

I began to think . . . that leisure activities are rather thin really. I mean there again, some weeks I do more than others, but this last week, I thought, Oh God, this looks as though all I ever do is go to meetings and come back home and eat and that's the end of it. But we did go out on Saturday night. (Adrienne Lyons, Labour Chair)

In spite of this evident lack of time, only a very few people seemed to think that their political activism had seriously affected pre-existing social relationships. Some said they saw their non-political friends less frequently; though others made a point of maintaining such friendships. Some said that casual socialising, like a chat with a neighbour or a morning cup of coffee with an acquaintance, had had to be cut out, but only one person claimed actually to have lost friends since becoming a councillor.

The extent of interference with leisure time varied – not surprisingly – according to the position the individual held within the community and the council. County councillors were more affected than parish councillors and other activists; and among those who held a council position, Chairs mentioned this problem more than backbenchers. Less obviously, there was also a party effect: Labour and Liberal councillors and party members – whatever their position – made more references to the consequences of their political involvement on their leisure time. Finally, women seemed to be more aware of the adverse effects than were men. Tying this in with the points we and others have made about women's leisure, we suggest that, in taking on the additional role of local politician, into an already full life, women may find that the concept of 'leisure' which is already a fairly nebulous one, becomes even more remote from their experience.

Undoubtedly, some of the people we spoke to (perhaps the majority) were quite content with this situation, at least for a time. This was particularly so for those who treated their community involvement as a vocation. Their commitment was such that they found it unnecessary to draw boundaries between their politics and their private life; as we have seen, their friends tended to share their beliefs, and their social and political lives were interwoven. If, however, they attempted to have any other outside activities, they – and their families – became increasingly frustrated.

This was the case with those, usually younger, Labour or Liberal party members and councillors, who were equally committed, equally likely to form close political friendships, and to involve their families in their work – but who wished nevertheless to treat their political work as a *job* with definite boundaries, yet found increasingly, as they progressed up the political ladder, that this was impossible. This tension between what they wanted and the existing situation was felt most acutely by women with families. They were concerned not only for their children, but also for their partners and their joint lives together; whereas men, it seemed to us, were more likely to regard their wives' unhappiness as regrettable but inevitable:

I'm sure Jane would say that she'd like to have more [leisure time] – particularly with me, I suggest. (Robin Scott, Labour Chair)

In contrast to this view, there are those who manage quite effectively to confine their political activities to a part of their life, only. We must not forget that community involvement is, in all senses, a *voluntary* activity. Joining a political party or a local community group often starts as a spare-time interest – and for some politicians it *remains* a hobby.

> I'm retired now and I have leisure all day long. As far as I'm concerned, my county council work is my leisure. I mean I can come back here [i.e. home] and have a snooze or a rest. (Leonard Wilson, Conservative Chair)

> I've got no hobbies, no interests. The only interest – well I say no hobbies, the hobby I've got obviously is politics, but I've got no interests . . . like most people would have a hobby of some kind, I haven't got anything at all. (Peter Mason, Labour back-bencher)

Overwhelmingly, those who took this position were men, and most were Conservatives. No female councillors and only a very small minority of women activists saw their community involvement as a 'hobby'.

In Chapter 7, we return to these three contrasting styles of political involvement, and begin to develop a model which links gender and party to political style or 'role' choice.

Always on call

Many of us have difficulty in drawing boundaries between our work and our leisure time. This, as we have suggested, is not exclusive to community activists, but applies to anyone who works from home, for example on a freelance basis, or caring for children or the elderly, or who may have an outside workplace but nonetheless regularly brings back work to do in the evenings and weekends. Many councillors, however, find they can rarely if ever demarcate periods of time solely for leisure purposes. As 'public' figures, they may be approached at any time, whether they are shopping in their local high street, weeding their gardens, having tea or relaxing in a hot bath before going early to bed.

I don't even find going to the pub and having a pint of beer is relaxation because invariably you get accosted by various people with problems. (Guy Davis, Labour backbencher)

For a few people, the fact that much of this work occurred when others were relaxing was a particular resentment, but most of them, especially those who had taken on a council position, took it for granted as part of the job. Margaret Winch, a senior Conservative member, said that even the telephone operators had noticed that she was always making council work-related phone calls on Saturdays and Sundays. And a Labour councillor (Gary Coulson) pointed out that weekends were 'a time when you can get hold of constituents, a time when they're free', and he therefore tried to allocate every other weekend to casework.

Inevitably, this level of commitment had considerable impact on their partners' lives. Margaret Winch's husband responded by developing his own interests in golf, reading and music; and both the Winches had decided that she would retire at the end of her current term. Mrs Coulson was in a less fortunate position, since her husband's way of life left her to cope alone with three very young children every other weekend. Partners also have to cope with direct intrusions into their lives – whether this comes in the form of abusive phone calls (which several spouses received) or simply continuous interruptions:

The inconvenience from 8 in the morning until midnight, you can always guarantee you'll get a phone call at some odd hour of the day. People knocking on your door, you can't walk to the shop without someone saying, 'Can your husband do so and so?' You know, it just tends to snowball after a while. (Mrs Tranter, wife of Labour backbencher)

Some councillors employed strategies such as unplugging the phone, having an unlisted number, getting their partner to answer (and if necessary say they are not at home), or simply saying firmly 'I never do anything on a Sunday – ring me tomorrow'. Some found that the only way they could get a break was to get out of the house, go away for a weekend, or longer if they could manage it. For example, one Labour Chair said that she always tried to go for a walk on Saturday afternoons, and then went out in the evening with her husband; another Labour woman (a backbencher) said that when she could not stand it any more, she arranged a weekend away with friends.

Partners, of course, can be very useful in helping to ensure that the activist gets an occasional break. They can also lighten the workload, or make it easier by, for example, taking messages, answering simple queries or diverting nuisance calls. In a few cases, where the partner was also active in the same political party, or on a council, he or she could deal with problems quite effectively. We came across one or two instances where a partner had built up such a good relationship with council officers that they were prepared to search for information or undertake work at the request of the partner when the council member was not available.

As we have seen, many political activists, and councillors in particular, are unable to be free of interruptions as long as they stay at home. Holidays away may therefore be even more important than they are for most people. In the case of council members, however, even holidays do not always provide a complete break from political commitments. For example, we met several councillors who had returned from their annual holiday for an important council meeting.

> I have travelled back from Wales when I've been on holiday to come back to meetings where I have important items on the agenda and I've been unable to spend two days holiday with [the family] or perhaps even the day after as well because I'm tired from travelling from the day before. But I've only done it three times over four years so really the effect is reasonably minimal. (Peter Mason, Labour backbencher)

Two councillors told us that at times the pressure of council business was so great that it was necessary to take council papers on holiday with them to ensure that they were adequately briefed for meetings on their return.

Councillors also faced other problems with respect to holidays, including whether or not they could manage to take them at all. Two councillors (both Labour) suggested that because of the length and frequency of council meetings, it was inevitable that they used up their holiday entitlement from their employment on council business. As a consequence, they did not have sufficient entitlement left to take a holiday. Other councillors remarked that it was difficult to find two consecutive weeks completely free of council-related commitments, even if (as in some cases) the month of August was kept more or less free of council meetings. This was a special problem for some women whose husbands had retired, and who preferred *not* to take their holidays at a time that most families with children chose to go, and when the price of accommodation and sometimes travel was inflated accordingly.

Financial considerations were also important to those who were worse off as a result of their voluntary community activities. One Labour councillor reported that council work so drained the family's financial resources that they were unable to afford a holiday. Linked to this was the observation by another councillor (again Labour) that there were no attendance allowances payable during August (when there were no meetings) and this made it financially difficult for her to take a holiday. Alternatively, if a councillor missed meetings to go on holiday, again s/he would lose the allowance because, unlike most people in paid jobs, councillors get no holiday pay.

Partnership or political widowhood?

We have already seen (in Chapter 4) some of the ways in which partners of political activists shoulder a heavier domestic workload because of their spouses' public commitments. At the same time, and unsurprisingly, many of them find that their leisure and social activities are seriously affected as well. Some partners were particularly vehement on this point:

> This is one of the things I wanted to say to you. One of the things that has really come about, and this is serious – *I* think it's serious, one of the things that has come about by her involvement as a county councillor is that we no longer do things together. (Mr Evans, husband of Labour Chair)

Since married couples frequently have joint friendships – perhaps inviting other couples round for a meal, or going out in a group for a drink, or to a theatre or restaurant – a heavy council workload inevitably affects the life of *both* partners.

While many partners were very supportive, they nevertheless sometimes resented a situation which was not of their own making, and in which – unlike the activists themselves – they were getting very few rewards for the sacrifices they were making. As one Labour Chair said, 'My husband gets quite bitter about it at times.' Other partners demonstrated their resentment more actively: we have already mentioned (Chapter 4) the husband who took advantage of his wife's absence to throw some of her council papers in a nearby skip, and another husband harangued one of us for three hours about his wife's iniquities. Wives, in contrast, were more inclined to express sadness than bitterness or anger. One woman, married to a senior Labour member, and with a long history of 'political widowhood' behind her, said sorrowfully that the quality of their relationship fell considerably short of what she would have liked, and compared badly with her friends' marriages. Two other wives, whose husbands held similar positions, said they never went out except to the shops and (in one case) her part-time job.

In examining these data, we have to bear in mind that the social consequences of being left alone in the evenings may be very different for women than for men. Apart from the need for someone to stay in with the children while they are young, there are other restraints on a woman's social life. For example, it is much harder for a woman to go to a pub, a restaurant or a party unaccompanied than it is for a man. This is partly a consequence of social pressures, but, added to this, many women fear sexual harassment or assault when going out at night. Going out with other women may reduce this fear but does not remove it altogether. Moreover, women friends may not be available in the evenings (perhaps because their own husbands control their leisure activities) and, if they are, transport may be a problem, since fewer women than men are able to drive, or have access to a car, and public transport in many districts is not available after 9 or 10 at night. In contrast, men, while often preferring their wives to accompany them on social occasions, are nonetheless not constrained in the same ways, and may comfortably enjoy a night out at the pub or with male friends. Men who have retired are perhaps more likely to miss their wives during the day – since, unlike women, they are not accustomed to spending their days in their homes alone – but we did not receive any specific complaints from men about restrictions on their evening social activities.

These gender differences relate in turn to different perceptions partners have of council-related social functions. We have seen how council members vary in their feelings about these occasions. Some see them as completely pleasurable, an enjoyable 'perk' of the job; others, as unavoidable but important occasions to make contacts or press a political advantage; others again see them as an utter waste of time and ratepayers' money. Partners' reactions are even more diverse. Quite often, it seemed that spouses were invited along to such functions, but wives were more inclined to accept than were the husbands of activists. There was some indication that whereas men can assume that their partners will almost automatically accompany them to such occasions, women need to negotiate this with their spouses, and when the men do attend, they do so in a rather grudging manner:

> I didn't go much on that. I didn't look forward to going. But when I go to these do's, you know, they usually turn out all right. (Mr Tutt, husband of Liberal councillor)

> Unfortunately, at times I'm forced to go. It's not my cup of tea at all, but yes, of course I've got to go and support her, you know, but those are things I object to because we've reached the sort of Saturday and Sunday stage now . . . there's civic Sundays and inauguration ceremonies and – oh God! – which really do take up a lot of time. Those are the sort of things that get me. (Mr Evans, husband of Labour Chair)

Because women's social life is, conventionally, more dependent on that of their husbands than vice versa, it may be that, in inviting his partner to accompany him, a male councillor or activist believes he is offering a kind of 'reward' for the patient uncomplaining home-based wife. For some wives, however, the value of such a 'reward' is questionable (and a few may reject it outright). More commonly, however, women will acquiesce out of a sense of duty, and on the implicit understanding that, for a man, appearing wifeless at such a function may stigmatise him and could damage his political career.

On the other hand – and in contrast to the 'normal' female situation – a female councillor or activist who is invited to a formal gathering in recognition of her public status, is not stigmatised by her spouse's failure to accompany her there. This seems to be an obvious example of the situation (referred to at the beginning of this chapter) whereby women 'create' leisure for men, sometimes at the expense of their own enjoyment. In consequence, male activists put considerable pressure on their wives to attend formal functions with them; and a woman who nevertheless refuses may be judged, and judge herself, more harshly for the same offence that many men are able to commit with equanimity. This is another example of the way in which women tend to be incorporated within their husbands' public lives, whereas, if the women herself is a councillor, the reciprocal process does not occur.

Do the children benefit?

If the benefits to the partner are problematic, those to the children appear – at least on the surface – to be less so. As we have said (Chapter 4) the majority of people we spoke to had had children, though some of them had now grown up and left home. There was wide agreement, among those councillors and other political activists who had had children under 16 living at home at some stage in their political careers, that their community involvement widened their children's knowledge and understanding:

> I like to be positive about it, and I like to think it's expanding her experience and I think this is something every parent has to decide . . . A lot of children are cut off from their parents' work experience. Whereas I think she is to a large extent aware of the sorts of things both of us are doing, and we try to explain and involve her. (Julia Freed, Labour backbencher)

> I think the eldest has got more of an awareness of what's going on locally by being within earshot of conversations. There's nothing harmful about that . . . And equally she seems to be taking on the same sort of role. She does various activities herself outside school . . . so that seems to have rubbed off on her in some way. (Mr Callan, husband of Conservative town councillor)

Other parents argued that their children gained social advantages from meeting a wide variety of people. This helped them to become more outgoing and confident in talking to people, and putting across a point of view.

> I would think they benefited because they've had more adults coming in and out of the house, and more discussions on political affairs, that kind of thing. (Mrs French, wife of Liberal councillor)

> He's aware of political leaders. He quite enjoys going to meetings. He's become a fairly outspoken child as opposed to any reserved part he had in him to begin with. He introduced himself to Neil Kinnock . . . He's very much aware for a four-and-half-year old. (Nina Parker, Labour candidate)

Conservative supporters were less likely than either Labour or Liberal activists to mention these kinds of benefits. They were also rather less likely to mention having political discussions in which their children joined. There was also a gender difference: women, whether they themselves were activists or the partners of activists, were much more inclined than men to point to the broadening effects of political life on their children. Perhaps women are more sensitive than men to these kinds of changes, or more aware of the potential impact of their actions, and those of their partners, on their children's lives.

A number of activists reported that their children were happy about their parents' involvement. Several children provided help of a practical kind – such as answering the telephone and taking messages – and some of them actively helped in delivering leaflets and campaigning.

> I think it does them good, they enjoy it. I mean if they didn't enjoy it, we wouldn't do it, but I think they do enjoy it. Peter delivers [leaflets] because at 16 it's all he can do at the moment, though we've promised him at this election he can sit on the polling station and say, 'Can I have your number please?' And Christopher does everything you tell him to. (Ann Leggatt, Liberal candidate)

Other children were more generally supportive and encouraging. Activists themselves sometimes made use of a 'happy family' image, by, for example, featuring family portraits on their election literature. Other parents, however, tried to keep their children away from the political side of their lives. Sometimes this was because they were aware of the potential dangers of indoctrinating them before they became familiar with alternative points of view. Others were wary of their children being seen as 'special' or different in any way. Attempts of this kind were not altogether successful, however. Once a parent became a public figure – such as a councillor – he or she was susceptible to adverse media attention, some of which also – directly or indirectly – affected the children. In a number of families, the children had been called upon to defend their activist parents. Moreover, some children had reportedly felt some embarrassment at reports in the press on their parents' public activities or speeches. In other families, pressure had been put on the children to 'behave themselves' in case a lapse reflected on the whole family.

The other negative consequence is clearly shortage of time. Children, as well as partners, clearly saw less of the activist parent than they would have done in different circumstances. We have already seen in Chapter 4 how women, in particular, would make time for anything 'really important'. They also argued – as do many working parents – that it was 'quality time' which was important and not simply the hours parent and child spend together. Men, on the other hand, tended to rely on their partners taking over all responsibilities. Only a minority felt their might be a real problem here:

The whole family, including me, doesn't go to the cinema, or out for meals, or to the theatre or to concerts and things. As a family, we don't do that at all, and the older ones have learnt how to get themselves to a concert or a cinema or theatre. (Jenny Anthony, Labour Chair)

I think it may have made them a little estranged, just a little . . . . Less affectionate, I think . . . . I felt that he was alienating himself from his children. (Mrs Wilson, wife of Conservative Chair)

In general, we feel that the people we talked to tended to play down the extent to which their community responsibilities interfered with their obligations to their families, and particularly to their children. We would certainly not wish to argue that parental political involvement is necessarily damaging to children. For children to grow up among people who take an informed interest in the world around them seems in principle to be beneficial; perhaps especially – because it challenges commonly held stereotypes – if the most active parent is the mother. Difficulties can, however, result from overload, leading in some cases to a sense of neglect and resentment in both the less active partner, and the children themselves. Looked at in this light, the almost universal denial by activists of any serious disadvantage to the children or to family life generally can perhaps be seen as an over-simple justification of a complex situation which was often far from perfect. This is underlined by the guilt which many activists (women in particular) confessed to experiencing.

The problem lies not so much with those individuals who attempt to combine family life with active community involvement (with more or less success) but with the expectations of those who defend the present system in the hope that sufficient individuals will come forward who are prepared to make crucial decisions for their local community, in their 'spare' time, and for almost no financial reward. This assumption – as with the lack of childcare facilities generally – based as it is on the belief that mothers will care for their children full-time for free, is not in tune with social changes (such as women's increasing involvement in the public world), and underlines the indifference with which our society treats the welfare of the next generation. It is also a further example of the way in which the call for greater diversity of political representation is not backed up by any practical measures to enable the ideal to become reality.

The social world of the councillor

A few previous studies have made passing reference to the links between council work and social life. For example, Elcock (1982, p. 73) following Rees and Smith (1964) notes that the council members' room often has a 'clubby' atmosphere which is enjoyed by some councillors. This phenomenon is also remarked upon by others (see Gyford 1984, p. 16) who puts the emphasis on the fact that party divisions can be less important than the sense of social unity created by being a councillor. In apparent contrast to this view, Jones (1969) in his study of Wolverhampton council, shows how social networks often form on a party-political basis, both within and outside the council chamber. These differences could, however, be a function of differences between the councils studied, in terms of size, type of authority, party composition and control. The writers may also be talking about rather different things. Many councillors will be generally friendly and sociable with each other regardless of party, but will look for practical support and friendship only from colleagues within their party group.

The extent to which social relationships and friendships are made through council work, and whether or not these are based on party lines, are questions we have addressed, but to which we can provide no final answers. A number of councillors said that they enjoyed the opportunity to socialise with members from all parties:

> I'm quite friendly with other members of the Tories and Liberals who you know are perhaps new councillors like me and are nice people in their own right. I may argue about politics but actually they are quite good company and you do spend a lot of time with them, having lunch between meetings and things like that . . . . They don't have this thing where they don't talk to you because you're in the Labour party or I don't talk to them but it's more an acquaintanceship than a friendship, they're pleasant people but nothing beyond that. (Sarah Hibbert, Labour Chair)

On the other hand, a smaller number – mainly Labour women – stated that they restricted their social contacts to members of their own party. Moreover, support and practical information – which newly-elected members particularly valued – was almost always provided by party colleagues. We tried to explore some of the reasons for these differing approaches. We wondered, for example, whether the extent of party-political domination within the council was a significant factor. If relationships between opposing groups are antagonistic, and if both groups are more or less equally balanced in size, members may choose to socialise only with others from the same party. On the other hand, if a member is in a very small minority party, she or he is likely to become friendly with some of the other members regardless of party group.

It's a Labour controlled county, Conservatives are very much in the minority, but a number of people came to me and helped me, regardless of political party . . . . It's not all that the press make it out to be, that we are all enemies; we're not. We're friendly people, I have made a lot of good friends, regardless of politics, in a short time. (Maurice Holmes, Conservative backbencher)

We did not, however, find any consistent patterns relating inter-party friendships to the party-political composition of the council.

Another possibility was that the people we were talking to were using the terms 'friendly' and 'friendship' in different ways. We tried to clarify this by asking first about socialising and 'friendly relationships', and secondly about 'close friends' (cf. Kurth 1970). When this distinction was made, some councillors said that it was important to them that their friends broadly shared their political beliefs:

Close friends . . . have to have the same outlook as yourself. Well, that's what I've found, anyway. I have certainly found people of different political persuasions stimulating to be with, but it would be difficult to have a close friendship with someone like that . . . . (Susan Tyler, Labour backbencher)

Those who felt this way – typically female Labour councillors – sometimes made friends with fellow councillors within their party group, but were in fact more likely to have initiated such friendships within their political parties before becoming a council member. Labour members, as we suggested earlier, have a long apprenticeship as party activists before putting themselves forward for election, and it is during this period that many close friendships are formed.

It is interesting, however, that Labour men were less inclined to stress the need for ideological compatibility in their close friendships. One, in particular, said that in principle, political considerations were irrelevant to friendship:

I've got friends right across the political spectrum, and I think that in many ways, when I pick my friends, I pick them because of their personalities, not because – I mean you become friends with them for other reasons. I've got people I've been friendly with since I've been at school and it happens they've become all sorts of shades of politics . . . (Ian Miles, Labour Chair)

Perhaps significantly, however, Mr Miles went on to add that 'because they're nothing to do with the Labour Party, I don't see them very much'.

It may be that women are looking for a greater degree of intimacy in their friendships than are men, and this level of closeness means that it is often important that friends share their values and beliefs. With such a small sample, it is impossible to be sure that this is a genuine difference between the sexes, though other research is also suggestive (Johnson and Aries 1983, Crawford 1977), and it also ties in with women's greater reliance on having a confidante (see Chapter 4, pp.95–6). These are certainly questions which could be fruitfully investigated in future studies of the sociology of friendship.

Friendships may also be based on gender, particularly for women, who are usually in the minority. On one town council for example, women of all parties often banded together as a group, and in this way managed to counteract some of the sexist comments (amounting to a mild form of harassment) which their presence provoked. A similar situation appears to exist in the House of Commons, according to press reports and informal conversations we have had with women MPs.

One reason why friendships within the council or with other party members may be so important is that many councillors find they have little time to maintain social ties with those who are not connected with politics. Moreover, for many of the most committed councillors, the political world becomes so central to their lives that their closest relationships are almost inevitably with those who share this understanding and commitment.

I'm on the council and I class that as my social life, because we have social evenings and all that, so that is my social life as well. (Harold Williamson, Liberal councillor)

In the light of comments like this, it was somewhat surprising that only two councillors saw their membership of the council as directly enhancing their social lives. When the discussion developed to explore the extent of socialising within the council and at council-related functions, however, many more councillors said that they now had more opportunities to develop social contacts:

> I do meet some very nice people. I also meet people I can't stand the sight of, but never mind. And various functions I go to because I'm a member of a local authority that we wouldn't go to otherwise. (Janet Baker, Labour Chair)

Nearly a quarter of the councillors we spoke to (most of whom held senior positions), put forward views of this kind. Not all these new friends and acquaintances are politically involved themselves. Local politicians are invited to a number of official and semi-official functions where they and their families meet a wider range of people than they might do otherwise. Some of them whole-heartedly enjoy this:

> You meet a lot of interesting people. Certainly people I wouldn't have met. A much wider range of people than I would have met living in a small town. (Leila Hilton, Conservative Chair)

> I think that is one of the rewarding things that kind of life gives you. You meet such wonderful personalities. Oh, I've met people from all over the world, royalty and all the rest of it . . . . (Bernard Chubb, Labour Chair)

Most councillors, however, distinguished, explicitly or implicitly, between this kind of social activity and their social life proper:

> I think inevitably you meet more people, if only the other councillors you know at meetings and things. You meet more people and one thing leads to another, all of which I suppose is a bonus if you like meeting people, but I don't think any of it has led onto making new friends. (Charles Rivendell, Conservative Chair)

Others dislike or are hostile to formal socialising, and may try to avoid all council-related functions, regarding them as a waste of time:

I don't go . . . . No, absolutely no, I dislike official functions. Been to one, that was enough. (Pauline Smith, Labour back-bencher.)

I think this involves a lot of members. You get involved in council work and there are social events, and frankly I do not approve of them, I never have, and as far as I'm aware I never will. I avoid them like the plague. (Barry Heightley, Labour backbencher)

While members of all parties were among those who enjoyed this kind of formal social function, those who disliked them were almost exclusively Labour and Liberal members. These differences were probably in part due to personal preference, and in some cases, formal functions could perhaps be seen as an escape from the bleakness and boredom of a councillor's private life. Over and above this, however, we suggest that the extent to which a councillor defined the member's role in partisan terms is likely to have a bearing on their willingness to attend official receptions as a representatives of the community. A Labour member who defines his or her role in political terms and is, moreover (as we have seen from workload figures) likely to have a somewhat heavier burden of council-related work than other councillors, is unlikely to be tolerant of purely symbolic activities. Labour women, whose private responsibilities particularly to the family are equally pressing, will find such occasions even more unappealing.

In apparent contrast, however, a significant proportion of this group are also 'political households' (as we have defined them in the previous chapter) in which political and social, private and public worlds intertwine for both the councillor and the partner. And, as we have seen, this can happen for certain other heavily committed political activists, as well:

There are leisure things that we actively go to . . . Much of our pleasure lies in party-based, Labour based [activities] . . . I mean it's terribly insular, you tend to find everybody tends to socialise within the group. Those are the things we tend to do if we're going out. (Janice Painter, Labour Chair)

You don't have a private life, if you're that involved, you really don't. That's what goes, your private life. All your social contacts tend to be with people in the party, simply because they're the people you meet all the time. (Jean Purdy, Labour candidate)

Most of our friends are probably largely in politics. I think probably we have very little or no social life which isn't tied up with politics in some way. (Mr Anthony, husband of Labour Chair)

The differences between this group and those who point to a wider range of social contacts stemming from council membership is more than one of degree. In the first place, the emphasis here is on political friendships with those of like mind. This tends to result in a narrowing rather than a broadening of social contacts. Secondly, the relationships which develop are likely to be deep and intense, in contrast to the relatively shallow but varied range of acquaintanceships in public life.

Once again, all these individuals were Labour members (over-whelmingly women) or their partners, reinforcing the points we have been making about the all-embracing nature of socialist politics for many Labour activists. This cannot fail to have an enormous impact on the social life and leisure of the rest of the family.

Conclusion: drawing boundaries between public and private life

In our lengthy discussions with councillors and other political activists as to the nature of their leisure and social relationships, a number of respondents observed that it was extremely difficult to separate the public domain of their lives from the private enjoyment of their social life and leisure. On the one hand, many of them experienced frequent interruptions to their private lives; on the other hand, council, political party and voluntary organisation membership generated friendships and extended social contacts, which could later include their partners as well. For many, their leisure and social life was inextricably bound up with their political life. The enmeshing of these two worlds could mean, however, that their genuinely private lives became extremely constricted; or in some cases, that the boundary between public and private worlds virtually disappeared.

As we have seen, there is a major distinction between the minority of activists (all male councillors) who see political work as part of their leisure, and the majority who see their public commitments as interfering in some way with their leisure and social activities. Most of those in the first category have low council workloads, and were backbenchers. The small number of Chairs in this category were able to accommodate their relatively high council workload because they were not in full-time employment, nor did they have school-age children at home.

The second category included councillors and other political activists of all parties – and none; though Labour and Liberal members were in the majority. The worst affected were female council Chairs, especially those with young children at home.

Most of those in this category were unable to distinguish clear boundaries between leisure activities and political work. Sometimes they found this rewarding; for example, when they made friends among their political contacts. Some regarded their political commitment almost as a vocation, to which they were happy to devote the whole of their lives. Others, however, were aware of the dangers of having too narrowly-focused a life. They believed that their own health and happiness and that of their families could be at risk if this situation continued for long. The women, who were the primary political activists in their households, would like to have treated their politics as a job – that is, as a predictable and time-limited commitment that allowed them to spend the rest of their time as they wished. The open-ended nature of the work, the demands of the public and the lack of adequate remuneration all made this impossible. Moreover, most of them were only able to cope with the continual pressures by relying heavily on the support of their partners (and sometimes their children) who in all cases shared their ideological commitment. Although this made the overall burden more manageable, it could nevertheless result in a situation where many women felt unable to escape from the relentless demands of their private and public lives. This has implications for widening recruitment and for turnover, which we will look at in Chapter 8.

6 Counting the Costs

I hope we can in some way in the future ensure that this commitment is analysed and looked at and some more rational system, I hope, arrived at whereby those who both have a job and the council are not seen in any way to feel guilty. (Ann Harris, Labour Chair)

Introduction

We now move on from family and social relationships to a consideration of the financial costs of being a council member. Any substantial voluntary commitment is likely to entail costs in terms of career advancement. There will not be the time to devote whole-heartedly to paid work; overtime may be forgone; and, in many cases, the activist may give up employment altogether.

As with the other issues we have looked at, the consequences are likely to be different for men and women. While, on the one hand, some women may feel more able to substitute political activism for a paid career, other women, in trying to balance the demands of their jobs and their families, and take on council work in addition, will face an even more complex task.

The allowances and expenses councillors can claim (under both the old and the new systems) fail to compensate for the income most members must forgo when they take on this demanding public role. How they cope with this situation is the subject of this chapter.

A conflict of interest?

Although a high proportion of councillors are in some form of employment (60 per cent in 1985) (Widdicombe 1986c, p. 28), the relationship between council work and paid work has received only cursory and incidental attention from official inquiries and academic researchers. More than twenty years ago, the Maud Committee offered the generalisation that young members in interesting jobs see council work as a supplement to their lives, middle aged members in more routine jobs may see it as a compensation and retired people tend to see it as a substitute (Maud 1967a, p. 139). On the issue of release from employment, a matter which had occupied the attention of a number of witnesses, the Committee concluded, somewhat unhelpfully:

> We are not in a position to assess to what extent the issue of release from employment is a serious difficulty for members nor to what extent it is a significant deterrent to people who might otherwise consider offering themselves as candidates. (Ibid. p. 147)

The question of a possible conflict of interest has preoccupied official inquiries. Both the Redcliffe–Maud Committee (1974) and the Salmon Commission (1976) recommended that local authorities should be required to maintain a register of councillors' pecuniary interests, including all paid employment. In 1975 the National Code of Local Government Conduct also made brief reference to professional business interests.[1] The Widdicombe Committee also made reference to councillors' employment in the context of a possible conflict of interest. It recommended that all councillors should be required to register any interests, including paid employment, which could reasonably be regarded as likely to affect his or her conduct as a councillor (Widdicombe 1986a). At the time of writing, the government proposes to require local authorities to produce a register of pecuniary interests of members in autumn 1990, but have not proceeded with the recommendation that members should make a declaration of non-pecuniary interests.

To date only one study has shown any understanding of the realities of being a councillor in employment. This examined the particular problems of the newly-elected member. What was the attitude of the employer?

> This will vary. Some firms will be proud that one of their employees is taking this step, they might see it as being marginally useful to the firm and might encourage the employee

to stand and provide the necessary support in terms of security of job and career. Other firms might agree but wish to guarantee that they will get the same amount of work out of the employee. Still others . . . may not be very encouraging at all and, although they may agree, it might be quite clear that career prospects in the firm would not be guaranteed if the employee becomes a councillor. (Fudge, Murie and Ring, 1979)

The present statutory rights of councillors to time-off for council work are embodied in Section 29 of the Employment Protection (Consolidation) Act 1978. This requires employers to permit employees to take 'reasonable' time-off for the purposes of performing duties as a councillor. This statutory right is limited, at least in principle, by two factors. First, there is no generally applicable statutory code of practice setting out what is 'reasonable', although, under the Local Government and Housing Act 1989, local government employees are allowed a maximum of 208 hours off per year. In contrast, there is such a code governing the equivalent provision for time-off for trade union activities. Nevertheless, it appears to be common practice for many employers in both public and private sectors to grant about eighteen days' paid leave per annum.

Secondly, there is no requirement to pay employees where time-off work is allowed. Research shows that a significant number of councillors suffer loss of earnings (Widdicombe 1986c). Both Robinson and Widdicome point to the dangers that financial hardship may inhibit individuals putting themselves forward for council membership, and this, in consequence, may help to explain the unrepresentative nature of local councils. The Robinson Report in fact established as a principle that

there should be no unnecessary impediment to the freedom of anyone to put themselves forward for election. Hence we think one important principle is that membership of local authorities should be truly open to all sectors of society without fear that it will entail financial hardship. (Robinson 1977, p. 35)

The Widdicombe Report makes clear, however, that there are councillors – not exclusively by any means manual workers – who do suffer financial loss, and as a result are penalised for their public service. Some years earlier, the Robinson Committee had commented that whereas the majority of those councillors in employment never lost earnings, a quarter always did and a further 15 per cent did so occasionally (Robinson 1977, p. 13). With respect to a councillor's pension rights, the Widdicombe Committee repeated the recommendation of the Robinson Committee that these should not be adversely affected by leave of absence from work (p. 137).

Expenses and allowances: the position before 1991

During the period of our research, the regulations governing the existing system of attendance allowances for local government councillors were those laid down in the Local Government Act of 1972 with some subsequent modifications in the Local Government, Planning and Land Act, 1980. Attendance allowances could be claimed by council members whenever they undertook 'approved duties' – which included attendance at council meetings, committee and sub-committee meetings, and could include other associated duties at the discretion of the local authority. There were variations between authorities as to what constituted 'approved duties'. Scottish authorities tended to adopt the most liberal interpretation of these duties. This may go some way to explaining why it is that members in Scotland received more than twice the average United Kingdom allowance figure.

The three councils in our study varied very slightly in their definition of 'approved duties'. None of them was among that minority of authorities that paid councillors allowances for attending party groups and constituency surgeries (Widdicombe 1986c, pp. 145–6). One of them allowed two half-days a month for attending to constituents' business at County Hall; and in all three authorities, certain senior councillors were allowed to claim for specified briefing meetings with officers.

The maximum rates of attendance allowance were prescribed by law and revised annually. The maximum daily rate in 1989–90 was £19.50 but this had not risen in line with inflation since 1973. An appropriate inflation-linked rate would now be in excess of £40 a day. Within that maximum sum, each council could determine what should be paid. Two of the three councils in our study paid the maximum rates whatever the duration of the 'approved duty' undertaken. The other council had three different rates depending on the time taken up. Attendance allowances were treated as earned income by the Inland Revenue, and were therefore taxable. It was possible to claim certain expenses as allowances against tax, but the councillors who mentioned this did not seem too happy about the way this concession operated.

Not all councillors actually took up attendance allowance. A significant minority (12 per cent) made no claim at all (Widdicombe 1986b, p. 113). Even for those who claimed, the sums involved were quite small: in 1985, 75 per cent of all councillors received less than £1000 per annum and 90 per cent received less than £2000 per annum (Widdicombe 1986b).

Both the Robinson and Widdicombe Inquiries were critical of the attendance allowance system. They felt that payment for attendance encouraged the proliferation of meetings (some of which might be unnecessary) and did not recognise the many aspects of the councillor's role. Instead, they recommended a system of flat-rate annual payments, topped up by a graduated system of special reponsibility allowances (SRAs) for senior councillors, scaled to the size of their authorities. They did not, however, advocate full-time 'salaries', even for selected senior councillors (see below).

One change put into effect as a result of the Robinson recommendations was the reintroduction of the 'financial loss allowance'. This could be chosen as an alternative (not an addition) to attendance allowances. It was not taxed, but acted as a reimbursement for those members who could demonstrate actual loss as a result of their council work. In our sample, only one councillor mentioned having exercised his right to choose financial loss allowance rather than attendance allowance, and for him the need to give notice, and the differing tax implications of the two forms of allowance, appeared to lead to complications. This is in line with the Widdicombe survey, which identified fewer than 1 per cent of councillors making this type of claim. The proposed new regulations (to be introduced in 1991) abolish the FLA completely for elected members.

Certain leading councillors may have been eligible for 'special responsibility allowances'. These were not mandatory (though under the new regulations they now are), nor was there any prescribed list of positions which attracted such an allowance. Widdicombe recommended raising these allowances and standardising them, rather than leaving them to the discretion of individual authorities, and this has, to some extent, now taken place (see Chapter 8). When the special responsibilities allowances were originally introduced, local authorities exercised considerable discretion in making them available to members. In 1985, only 43 per cent of local authorities provided special responsibility allowances for their members. Almost all Scottish authorities, London boroughs and metropolitan counties introduced them, but very few of the shire counties did so. As one would expect from this geographical variation, Labour-controlled counties were more than twice as likely to pay this allowance than were Conservative-controlled authorities, perhaps reflecting the greater needs of their members (Widdicombe 1986c, p. 136).

Where an SRA was paid, it was an annual sum (not related to attendance), it was taxable, and it tended to be paid to such councillors as Chair and Vice-Chair of the Council, and Chair of major committes (such as Education and Social Services), and occasionally to the leaders of the ruling party group and the main opposition parties. Most of these points apply to the new SRAs also.

What do allowances mean in practice?

We did not ask any of the people in our study directly about the financial costs of their activities. Nevertheless, most of the councillors we spoke to commented on the financial implications of their council membership, both directly – in terms of expenditure and income forgone – or indirectly, as it affected their paid employment. Most of their remarks were critical, either of the level of allowances paid, or of the apparent lack of understanding of those who expected them to combine, easily, a full-time job and a council career.

The Widdicombe researchers detected widespread unease among councillors about attendance allowances across all parties more or less equally. Within our study, criticisms of attendance allowances came from councillors of all parties, but from rather more Labour members than Conservatives. It may be that they were more dependent on these allowances than many of the Conservatives and Liberal members we spoke to; or perhaps they were more inclined to regard the payment of councillors as a right, rather than a privilege. Complaints tended to focus around three basic issues: the rates of payment, the rigidity and arbitrariness with which the rules for payment were applied, and the implications posed for tax liabilities and eligibility for state benefits.

It's not enough to live on. It depends how many committee meetings you have, but if you're unfortunate enough to have three in a day, you see, you get paid £16 because it isn't per meeting, it's per day. So hopefully most of mine fall on different days of the week. I've heard people say you shouldn't regard it as employment. For tax purposes, [though] it is regarded as employment. I certainly wouldn't do it for nothing because everybody has got to eat, you know. (Susan Tyler, Labour backbencher)

Contrary to what people think, unless you attend County Hall a great deal, you only get paid for attendance at County Hall, every single thing else you have to pay out of your own pocket. (Eleanor Mansfield, Liberal backbencher)

Only a few councillors, in contrast, made approving comments about attendance allowances. These were mostly members who received them in addition to their salaries (which for them were paid in full whether they took time off or not) or who were non-employed with employed partners, and for whom, therefore, the attendance allowance was a bonus they would not otherwise have received.

The registered unemployed, on the other hand, faced particular difficulties, as did those married to unemployed partners. Some unemployed councillors found they had problems in signing on as 'available for work' because they made known their council commitments. Those who had been unemployed for more than a year were dependent on Supplementary Benefit (now Income Support) which was means tested, and therefore they lost almost all this benefit when they received attendance allowances. Benefits for dependents are also means tested, which put one Labour woman councillor in a very difficult situation:

The first time [my husband] was unemployed, . . . they could only pay him single-person dole, because if I had one meeting at County Hall, it was . . . more than they would have paid him if he'd claimed for me. When his dole ran out, I naturally thought he'd be entitled to Social Security but he wasn't. Some weeks, I only had two meetings, three at the most, say £40, and we had an awful job, with £20 rent rebate . . . . And when I went to tell the [housing benefit office] they said that they couldn't understand that I wasn't paid on a regular basis, and they couldn't take the weeks when I had no money into account. I tried to explain [that they should average it out] but I got so fed up that in the end I didn't bother . . . (Barbara Morgan, Labour Chair).

Mrs Morgan went on to add that 'It's hard enough being a man councillor if you're out of work, but if you're unemployed and married to a woman [councillor] it's even worse.' Fortunately, Mr Morgan didn't appear to resent this situation – as many men would have done – but the financial problems this couple were faced with until he found another job were a considerable strain on their relationship.

The Widdicombe researchers (1986b) argued that even if allowances were increased significantly and the tax and social security anomalies were sorted out, any system based on attendance allowances is inappropriate because many of the duties do not entail attending formal meetings. They go on to claim that there is now more support, albeit from a small minority of councillors, for the payment of a full salary to members. They further claim, however, that even if a majority reject the notion of a full-time salary, there is considerable support for some kind of 'salary equivalence' for leading members and this was seen as preferable to the special responsibility allowance. This would only be feasible, however, if it was set at a level which would allow the council member to give up his or her employment. Also, in view of the considerable variation in council workloads (documented in Chapter 3) we feel that any flat rate payment, whether as 'salary' or otherwise, needs to be modified in accordance with hours put in. At the time of writing, the implications of the Local Government and Housing Act in respect of allowances to councillors are not completely clear. (See Chapter 8 for further discussion.)

In addition to attendance allowances, councillors may also claim travelling expenses from their home or place of work to County Hall or the equivalent, and subsistence allowances are also paid if they are away from home for a period of (usually) four hours or more. No other expenses – e.g. telephone or postage costs – may be claimed, as the attendance allowance is supposed to cover them; though one of the authorities we looked at did give some of their senior councillors a telephone credit card, and paid the rental on the telephone for other members. Mileage payments were generally quite low – varying from 10p to 17p a mile, which barely covered the cost of petrol, and compared badly to mileage rates paid by other organisations at that time.

Some councillors felt that council membership was also responsible for a number of extra costs. A particular expense was often a second car, which would not otherwise have been necessary:

> We have to have two cars. We've been with only one for the last fortnight and it's murder trying to cope. There have twice been occasions when we've hired a car just because we can't really cope . . . . I need a car in the evenings as well, and my husband, even if he isn't going out himself, there's usually a child to be taken somewhere . . . . (Marian Gaines, Liberal county councillor)

One interesting finding was that, whereas male councillors felt it was acceptable to commandeer the 'family car' for council business or employment, and leave their wives at home without one, female councillors, who needed a car for their council work, were most insistent that their husband, even if retired or unemployed, could not be left at home without one.

Priorities: the council versus employment

As we have seen, council attendance allowances have been very low, and were only paid in any case for 'approved duties'; whereas much of the work council members do does not come into this category. Because of this, most councillors were unable to manage financially if they were totally reliant on attendance allowances. Many of them, therefore, had to keep on with their paid employment. This meant, though, that they often had to make difficult decisions regarding the relative importance of their (unpaid) council commitments and their (paid) job.

We spoke to councillors about their priorities, and of those commenting, just over half put their council work first. There was a clear gender difference here. Women, particularly those who were married, tended to give the highest priority to council work; and some of them had given up their employment as their council commitments grew. This decision, which was the result of the difficulties of combining the two jobs, was explained by two senior councillors in the following terms.

In point of fact I gave [my job] up because I couldn't manage to do the two. It was too much for me and I enjoyed county work. I was [working] in a hospital and it began to worry me because I realised I wasn't giving it the attention that I should have done. I was sort of split and I did resign because I wanted to go on doing council work, so it was a conscious decision. But you see, because of that, it's cost me thousands of pounds. (Janet Baker, Labour Chair)

Well, I used to work part-time until about four years ago, and then I found, quite honestly, that I was so often rearranging my time to fit the council that it was no longer practical for me to continue. But I used to work twenty hours per week. I dropped it to sixteen and then gave it up. But, quite honestly, with the amount of time and effort that goes into this sort of work, I find it quite stressful . . . . (Catherine Thorne, Conservative Chair)

Candidates were even more emphatic than existing councillors that council work and paid employment could not be combined. Several of them expressed the intention of giving up their jobs if they were elected. Others said that they preferred political and council work to any paid job they might do, and other felt that politics was such an important part of their lives that they regarded it as a career-substitute (see below).

No, I wouldn't keep my job on after the election . . . . The way council meetings are arranged, and with the trade I'm in, I couldn't do it. (Maureen Fowler, Labour candidate)

In contrast, men, if they expressed any priority at all, tended to put their employment first. These two Conservatives for example, both in employment, had no hesitation:

> If I get crises at work . . . well, probably they take precedence . . . well, business takes precedence . . . . (Richard Hall, Conservative Chair)

> Over the last year or so, since we have been building this factory and increasing the size of it and so on, I really haven't had an awful lot of time that I could devote to things like that and, because I've had meetings here and recently because of the chaos that ensued when we altered this factory, I've been here seven days a week . . . . I have to earn a living. (Jeremy Austin, Conservative backbencher)

No less emphatic was an unemployed male councillor:

> I've made a decision that if a job comes along that will require my stepping-down from the council, then I step down from the council. I've got to earn a living. I've got children. I can't live on Social Security – no one can. If the choice is between a job and staying on the council, I go for the job. (Gary Coulson, Labour Chair)

In addition to this gender difference, there was a small party difference. Conservative councillors were rather more likely to give priority to employment and rather less likely to put council work first. The majority of councillors who were not able to express a clear priority said that it would depend on the circumstances they found at any particular time.

Job loss

Many councillors expressed concern about the effect of council work on their future careers. A number of people mentioned either the loss of promotion prospects or the difficulty in getting future employment. This corroborates the finding of research commissioned for the Widdicombe Inquiry:

Among the respondents to the Social and Community Planning Research survey, there were relatively few who had apparently either lost their jobs or resigned their jobs as a direct result of holding office on a local authority. But, for every individual who has been sacked or forced to resign, there must be many who felt threatened or have felt their future promotion prospects likely to be damaged. Several such instances were cited to us, often in quite an off-hand manner, as if the situation was only to be expected. (Widdicombe 1986b, p. 52)

The greatest conflict of priorities arises when a councillor runs the risk of losing his or her job involuntarily. One instance of this was mentioned by one male councillor whose working life had become increasingly problematic as his council commitments increased. When he was with an earlier employer difficulties were apparent:

> [Inflexible hours] was one of the reasons . . . but I saw that it was difficult because of the position I was then occupying with them. I was sort of field work manager . . . and therefore it was important to be on the job most of the time and because they were all over the south west . . . and therefore to get back for an Education meeting which was an all-day event . . . I knew the difficulty. (Robin Scott, Labour Chair)

The breaking-point was reached when a later employer wanted him to work 'standard' hours:

> I mean originally when I joined them they gave me a flexi-hours arrangement that suited me and presumably suited them. [Then] they said . . . that they wanted me to work the same hours as most of the other staff were working, and that wouldn't be possible while remaining a councillor and, though they said they'd like me to stay on, it just wasn't feasible. (Robin Scott, Labour Chair)

Mr Scott's position was different from that of either Janet Baker or Catherine Thorne (quoted earlier) since he clearly believed he had been forced out by his employer's apparent change in the terms of his contract. Other councillors had also experienced involuntary job-loss as a direct or indirect result of their council commitments.

Promotion and future job prospects

The consequences were only slightly less severe for those members who told us that they had had to forgo promotion because of their council position. Most of them were Labour men in clerical, supervisory and manual occupations. The following comment is typical.

> I can think of four specific occasions when one was approached to consider certain options and the obvious question that I'm obliged to ask them is about time off . . . so you back away . . . . Now I lost a job I felt I could do . . . . I felt a little upset in March . . . . There's a job and my wages are five-and-a-half-thousand pounds a year and this one would have taken me over seven. (Ronald Jones, Labour Chair)

Another councillor saw promotion as being dependent on giving up council work:

> In fact quite a few of my colleagues have had promotion during the last two years and part of that promotion was that they had to give up council membership at the next election, so the last election has just gone . . . there was at least three who had to give it up because of promotion. In the job you have to weigh up whether you want promotion or public life. Promotion comes once or twice. Public life is there. But if you turn promotion down, as I say, you're only as good as your next ballot paper. If that goes the other way you've lost both sides. (Jim Pearson, Labour backbencher)

We were not in a position to establish the veracity of these claims concerning lost promotion. It would have been extremely difficult to determine whether employers *did* systematically discriminate against their employees who were councillors in the way that has been alleged. Nonetheless, these allegations are consistent with a general pattern of employer ambivalence which is reported throughout this chapter.

Prospects of future employment also might have been harmed. A number of councillors who had no paid employment at present said that they had misgivings about the future. For example:

I think that after being on the County Council it would be a very difficult situation because you know quite a lot about certain things but as I said you're not qualified and other people can then regard you as a bit of a know-all. I think it's like MPs. When they lose their seat they often find great difficulty in getting work and I think people are suspicious about you. (Barbara Morgan, Labour Chair)

Labour women were particularly likely to voice such fears. How can we account for this? As we have indicated, among women councillors, a high proportion were non-employed. In this group, all the Conservatives were over fifty, whereas amongst the Labour and Liberal councillors, many were under fifty, including all but one of the women who complained about reduced employment prospects. Is this difference merely what could be expected, in that older women are, unsurprisingly, less concerned with their employment prospects than younger women? This may be the case. Alternatively, the difference may be *generational*, i.e. that younger women view the loss of employment with much greater concern than the earlier generation of women councillors. If this interpretation is valid, it has clear implications, in the medium term, for the recruitment of women as local councillors. (See below for further discussion.)

Managing the twin burdens

Comments by employed councillors on how they manage their workload were predominantly critical or complaining in character. They reflected three related difficulties: those arising from the *volume* of work; those arising from the lack of *time*; and those arising from attempts to *compensate* for time lost in employment. The total volume of work to be done, together with a general shortage of time, were frequently mentioned by those who were currently employed. In respect of their paid jobs, this overload was attributed to two main factors: variations in the amount of work to be done (due to seasonal fluctuations, factory rebuilding, the demands of clients, etc.); and secondly, to the particularly demanding nature of some forms of employment. The following comment provides an illustration of this sense of overload.

I do deal with litigation, which is court work, and I had a large number of big cases coming up during 1984 and I did find it extremely difficult at times during that period from the spring onwards until about September time . . . It was very difficult. (Mervyn Prescott, Liberal)

Some councillors reacted to a large workload by curtailing their council commitments. This was done by choosing to sit on only a small number of committees, or, alternatively, on the less-demanding ones.

Apart from a general shortage of time, (which is explored in Chapter 3) difficulties arose for some councillors from the time-tabling of council activities. Councillors who worked night-shifts or 'unsocial hours' were most affected. One night-shift worker had difficulty exercising his right to time-off because no council meetings were held in the middle of the night! After many months of negotiation a compromise was reached:

For meetings at [County Hall] I have no problem. I just put a leave of absence in to come home at 1.30 in the morning and then when I get to [County Hall] I have a form . . . I fill it in myself, you know . . . all I ask them to do is to sign it . . . but I think it's embarrassing. (Peter Mason, Labour backbencher)

Others felt it would be better for them to spread their committee meetings throughout the week, rather than have two (with a lengthy midday break) on the same day:

Yes, it is awful uneven . . . I did have two meetings on the same day and they've stopped that, where I had one at eleven and one at two. But obviously that meant that I had to finish work at ten and I wouldn't get back to work until four, and it was too long on a regular basis to cover my time. (Josephine James, Labour Chair)

Some members spoke about how they compensate or make up for the time lost at work. This group divided equally between doing work in the evenings and at the weekends, and those who used at least part of their holiday entitlement to catch up. This comment from one of the small number of employed Conservative women councillors reflects a common feeling that the norm of eighteen days off a year is inadequate.

I have eighteen days' paid leave a year which I can take for council work or council-related work. It would be the same if I was a JP, and also, if I became Mayor or something like that, they would give me secondment for a year. So those are laid-down regulations. That was agreed when I took up this present post and it was agreed when I was first on the council. So that's it. But I also take at least a week of my paid holiday for council business. That's why you have to be careful because eighteen days doesn't go very far. Eighteen days isn't sufficient. Oh, the only other time I can create half-days is by working Saturday mornings. So when I'm on call I will work the Saturday morning and take it in lieu, which will create another half-day for me . . . . That situation is quite useful . . . but it doesn't help much . . . . It's six half-days a year. So I have to be careful. (Carol Stothard, Conservative backbencher)

Those who were self-employed were to some extent more flexible in the time they could have off, but this was not without its consequences. Hugh Fordham, for example, employed a reliable full-time manager – at considerable expense – to run his farm in his absence. Maureen Porter was able to call on her husband to help run her business when she had a council meeting on a day her part-time assistant was not there – but this meant that he was unable to carry out his own work in another side of the same business, so they lost income through it. Mr Peel – whose wife was a Conservative candidate – insisted that her business was now running at a loss rather than a substantial profit because of her lack of input; though Mrs Peel herself insisted that business would have declined anyway, and there was no problem at all.

'Of course I can't take a job': council work as career substitute

A quarter of the councillors we talked to saw council work as a replacement for a career in paid employment, in the sense that it had acquired a prominence similar to that of paid work in many people's lives. The majority of these councillors were not currently employed full-time, or were approaching retirement, and/or in jobs where they could see no career advancement. In all cases, council work provided a satisfaction which was greater than that received from their employment, or from any job which they could realistically aspire to hold. There was a noticeable gender differ-ence in the patterns of career replacement: the women did so after a change in domestic circumstances, e.g. child-care. Some of these women chose not to take up employment again; others after a break were unable to find suitable paid work. The men did so after retirement or redundancy. The women's view was exemplified by these statements:

> I mean, it was something I could do that would fit in the family and responsibilities that I had at that time. (Doreen Grey, Conservative Chair)

> The alternative would have been to have trained and to have looked for some paid employment but it would have been exceptionally difficult with the hours that my husband works. (Leila Hilton, Conservative Chair)

Council work can be a job-substitute at different phases of women's lives: for some (e.g. Doreen Grey above) it was after the children had grown up; for others, as in the following example, it was while they were young after which other activities might gradually take over.

> It was the first sort of satisfying outside work I've done since having the children and I think there are always advantages in having something that's outside the family, so in a sense it had a lot of the advantages that I would've had if I'd gone out to work in an ordinary job. (Jenny Anthony, Labour Chair)

Several women (all Labour or Liberal) whose children were growing up and who had unsuccessfully sought paid employment, now stated a preference for council work.

> I really enjoy being a councillor and, having tried to get paid work and failed, and thrown myself into council work a lot more . . . . It isn't just being on the county council, it's also the district council because I've taken on a lot of extra responsibilities there, and I find that totally satisfying. So I wouldn't want to go back to paid work because it would involve giving up something of what I was doing and I'm quite convinced that I wouldn't get anything that was very interesting anyway. (Marian Gaines, Liberal)

Unlike the Conservative women – most of whom were older – these were all women who had initially wanted to go back into a paid career, but limited job opportunities in their areas led them to the view that council work was preferable, or precluded altogether the option of a paid job. Some of them, while seeing their council work as a 'job', regretted that, as it was not paid, other people did not recognise it as such:

> I do resent the fact that [the children] do expect the house to be my responsibility. Once they get to the age they are, I quite honestly don't see why it should be. This is one of the problems of being a councillor – the working mums. It's accepted that working mums go out to work, but if you're a councillor . . . they tend to think you're not a working mum. (Marian Gaines, Liberal councillor).

> [My husband] had a thing that people only value you if you do a paid job and that perhaps you only value yourself. (Rosalind Litton, Labour Chair)

One husband also commented on the significance of his wife's involvement in council work:

> She could have contributed to the family income by getting employment but she never did and when she got elected to the

county council . . . she then had her identification . . . she had a role to play. She then had her status. She had prominence and she was therefore quite taken up with this in a very, very big way and therefore she had a role to play and she had a job to do.

These remarks express two closely related anxieties – financial loss and ambiguity of status, which are related to the demands that are made upon these (female) councillors by members of their own families. The fact that council work is not paid work analogous to that of MPs, managers, and professionals seems to bear most heavily upon younger women with families – a section of the adult population which is statistically under-represented on local councils throughout the country.[2]

For the men, the lack of proper payment for council work often made it even harder for them to consider giving up their jobs. For some of them, however, the prospect of retirement could precipitate an interest in council work as a potential substitute for the career that was now drawing to an end. The following two men had worked or were still working in managerial or professional positions.

Well, [the work] does fluctuate – of course it does. It doesn't always come at the right time. But being retired I can adjust to it. I don't think I could have . . . there is no way I could have taken this on while I was still in business. There's no way I could do justice to it. There are people who run their own businesses. There are people who are in work who operate as councillors and they seem to manage, but quite frankly I don't see it that way. (Maurice Holmes, Conservative backbencher)

I didn't want to sit at home doing nothing. I like to be involved and I was persuaded that at last I could devote the necessary time to the council and that I could do it . . . . I did try to get clarification of whether I would or would not take early retirement before I finally put my name forward. I hung on in an indecisive way as long as possible but eventually I had to persuade myself that I could do the task and work here as well. But it is quite clear that I could spend an awful lot more time than I do. (Paul Jackson, Conservative backbencher)

For other male councillors, unemployment in the course of their working life was the circumstance which gave rise to career-replacement. The advantage of having time was still appreciated. But to be without work involuntarily could also have its drawbacks:

> **Interviewer**: Do you think that the fact that you're not employed is an advantage or a disadvantage?
> **Councillor**: Well, it's got advantages and disadvantages. The advantages are that I've got more time to do research . . . and I can call on more constituents than I could have during work time. The disadvantage is the absence of working colleagues . . . . There is this other aspect you know. [Council] colleagues recognise I'm in this situation and they tend to lean on you and abuse the fact that I'm in this situation and I keep warning them that I'm still looking for a job. (Barry Heightley, Labour backbencher)

> I have applied for several jobs since and in fact I applied for one yesterday. If I get a job then I will seriously have to consider the situation as to whether I could carry on doing both jobs efficiently . . . . (Tim Meeson, Labour backbencher)

Only in one instance amongst the female councillors was career replacement directly related to changes in her employment rather than domestic circumstances. This arose when her work in a large multinational company was transferred to another part of the country. Her husband did not want to move and she was, as a result, compelled to give up her job. In neither interview did she describe the circumstances which gave rise to her council work, but her husband responded at length:

> We got to the stage where my wife was in the finance department at [company] . . . and they were moving the staff from South-town to Northtown and she came home and we seriously discussed it because at this time I personally was away as much as I was at home . . . whether she would go to Northtown or not. I certainly didn't want to live in Northtown . . . but on the other hand she did have a career of her own, we didn't have a family . . . and in the end she decided no, she didn't want to go to

Northtown. She wanted to stay here and put up with what time I was able to come home. Then she was in a bit of a vacuum in the sense of what she was doing with her time. She didn't honestly believe that she could sort of sit and be a *hausfrau* and I'm not being condescending in saying that it just wasn't her nature. (Mr Evans, husband of Labour Chair)

Patterns of career-replacement were not, in general, party-linked. Some councillors said, however, that council work provided interest (and a little income) at a time when job opportunities were few. Of those who had made this kind of comment, only one was a Conservative who had subsequently found work. All the others were Labour or Liberal women who appeared to place little emphasis upon material gain.

Having served on the council, how I'll find employment I don't know. I suppose basically I'm not a careerist. I don't feel very upset that my working life has been interrupted by this. I tend to work from what comes up. I'm a great believer that opportunities do arise. By doing this for the council I've been building up all sorts of skills that I wouldn't otherwise have – getting more contacts, getting more information that just wouldn't have come my way – so I think, you know . . . it's not a negative experience in terms of the jobs I might apply for in the future . . . . I'm against full-time work anyway, it's just unhealthy for most people. I might envisage in the future that I might do a small number of small amounts of work which would add together to the equivalent to a part-time job or three-quarter time job. I don't know . . . we'll have to wait and see. (Julia Freed, Labour backbencher)

There was a certain amount of resentment started in the family that I was spending all my time running around and we were short of money and why wasn't I earning money? So I thought, why didn't I go back to work? . . . I got really into a state of depression. I kept applying for jobs . . . [and] I couldn't get a job of any description apart from [in the fish and chip shop]. I suspect being a councillor had something to do with it, because I've talked to other people who tried to change jobs and they haven't been able to. (Marian Gaines, Liberal councillor.)

Labour and Liberal women like these entered the council hoping to go back into employment in future, and only changed their minds, if at all, at a later stage. Conservative women, in contrast, were more likely to make council work their first choice.

Conclusion: the cost of council membership

Clearly, in many cases, the costs of council membership are very high. Because of the difficulties of combining full-time paid employment with council position, many of the people we spoke to had cut back on their working hours, or given up their jobs, or were considering doing so. Others had lost promotion or had been given warnings by their employers, and at least one had been dismissed from his job when he became a candidate. Council work itself also has direct financial costs, which were not adequately compensated for by attendance and financial loss allowances.

There seemed to be a division between those who could afford these extra direct and indirect costs of council membership, and those for whom any loss or potential loss of income was a serious matter. The first group was mainly older, had partners earning a sufficient income, or were self-employed or retired, and tended to be Conservatives. Most of the second group relied on their earnings to provide for themselves and their families. If they were non-employed, their children were young and needed full-time care which had to be paid for in some way if the mother took on a serious daytime commitment.

Among councillors, there was considerable support, particularly among Labour members, for the idea that council members should be paid a proper salary. Candidates were less inclined to favour this solution, however – perhaps because at this stage they had not fully realised the implications of council membership. It may be, however, that others, who are more aware, fail to come forward because they are not prepared to make the necessary financial sacrifices.

In the White Paper preceding the 1989 Local Government and Housing Act, the Government argued that there was no need for significantly increased allowances or salaries for councillors, because they saw no evidence of a shortage of candidates (Department of Environment 1988, p. 9). In contrast, our earlier

discussion of recruitment, supported by other evidence, demonstrates that in certain parts of the country, there is an acute
shortage of potential candidates, particularly from certain occupations and social groups. In our view, the prospects of widening the
pool of potential council recruits are very limited so long as local
politics is seen as a voluntary part-time commitment. In our final
chapter, we return to this problem and discuss some possible
solutions.

Notes

1. Issued as Circular 94/75, Department of the Environment, 1975.
2. In 1985, women under the age of 44 were statistically under-
   represented (in relation to the adult female population) and women
   over that age were over-represented (except for the over-75s). See
   Widdicombe 1986d, Tables 2.1 and 2.4.

PART IV
THE PRIVATE FACE OF POLITICS

7 Political Styles

Introduction

It is clear from earlier chapters that what the councillor does is related to how he or she defines the job to be done: how much time is to be devoted to policy issues, how much casework to take on, how to manage links with the party, how to react to local pressure groups, and so on. In this chapter we focus on these and other related issues and present a model of three political styles which provides an understanding of the complex and intertwined public and private worlds of the elected member. These styles treat council work as a hobby, as a vocation and as a job. The distinguishing criteria in each case include hours of work, the predominant nature of the work and the balance councillors perceive between their public and private worlds. These styles tend to develop along lines of gender and party.

A choice of roles?

In working out their own private answers to these (and other) questions councillors are not, of course, completely free to do as they like. Inevitably, they are under some sense of obligation that they should perform their duties in certain ways. In so far as most councillors today, for example, have been elected as representatives of a political party, then the party in question (both inside and outside the council) can be expected to influence how they carry out their duties. Moreover, each council evolves its own unique pattern of constraints or 'rules of the game' some of which are defined by legislation but most of which are simply social or conventional in character. These also limit the extent to which each individual member is free to decide the nature of the task to be done.

Within this framework of social convention and legal limitations, the councillor develops a style which expresses her or his civic and political purpose and which represents an attempt to reconcile the many conflicting demands which arise from family responsibilities and employment. What the councillor does is not, therefore, simply determined by the expectations coming from the public world of council chamber and party group, but also by constraints coming from the private world of marital and family relationships, social and leisure activities, employment and the expectations that each councillor brings to the task.

As we have suggested earlier, previous studies of the roles of elected members have focused simply on the public world – that is, the councillor's ward, length of service, seniority and party allegiance (Budge *et al.* 1972, Dearlove 1973, Heclo 1979, Newton 1976, Lee 1963). Our approach has been much broader in taking the councillor's private life into consideration, also. Moreover, in talking to councillors and their partners, we were careful to avoid predetermining the answers to our questions. Those we talked to were free to respond as they wished to our questions.

The councillor as policymaker

In spite of the considerable shortcomings we mentioned in Chapter 3, the Widdicombe Report provides the most up-to-date information available on the policymaking role and other roles of councillors. Local politicians, as we have seen, may interpret their duties in a variety of ways. They will react differently and attach differing importance to the many groups and individuals with whom they have contact – local constituents, party members or council officers. In the light of their varied interests, abilities and domestic and employment situations, the range of possible interpretations are considerable. One major distinction is, however, between those councillors who see themselves as policymakers and those who see themselves as primarily concerned with casework.

It is clear from the Widdicombe interview survey that there is a tendency for those senior councillors whose interests lie in debating and determining the main policy guidelines for the authority to talk impatiently and disparagingly of members who 'are only interested in their own patch' and who appear as a consequence to contribute little to the committee work and policymaking process of the authority. These are the 'makeweight councillors' who leave the major questions of policy to a small group of leading members. Typical comments made by these councillors in response to the Widdicombe interviewers were:

My life would be much easier if we didn't have quite so many members.

It would be much easier to manage this authority with fewer members. (Widdicombe 1986b, pp. 56–7)

The findings of the postal questionnaire, however, indicate that members widely support a policymaking role for local authorities and their members. They were asked, for example, to react to the following statements:

The most important role of local government is to represent the interests of the people in the area.

It is for local councillors rather than central government to determine local needs and priorities.

In respect of both statements, more than 90 per cent of councillors either agreed or agreed strongly. A third statement,

Back-bench members have little real influence over decision-making

produced a much less polarised response with 27 per cent agreeing and 43 per cent disagreeing (Widdicombe 1986c, p. 65).

In our own investigation of county councillors, it was the Labour members in the two counties which were Labour-controlled who made most comments on policymaking. We received no comparable comments from Conservative governing group members of the third county council. The comments from the Labour members came equally from backbenchers and chairs. In response to the question, 'In your view what are the most important aspects of your job as a councillor?', a representative comment was:

Being able to put through socialist ideas and being able to carry out true socialism into your everyday activities as a councillor and that is helping people who are deprived both on a materialistic point of view – deprived from all sorts of view . . . . (Adrienne Lyons, Labour Chair)

Labour members were also preponderant amongst those who spoke of the need to specialise and concentrate on the affairs of one committee.

You cannot serve on all the committees effectively. You've just got to be the noddy man on some of the committees . . . . (Gary Coulson, Labour Chair)

If policymaking and specialisation were aspects of the roles of Labour members, what were the views of Conservatives and Liberals with regard to the part they saw themselves playing in the business of the council? As we remarked in Chapter 3, only a minority of councillors saw attendance at council meetings as a significant part of their council workload and of these most were Conservative or Liberal. Apart from this, Conservatives said very little about the way they chose to operate within the council. The absence of comment suggests that this aspect of the councillor's role is generally unproblematic for Conservatives. Why is this? Is it related to their lower workloads? (See Chapter 3.) Or is it, as we are inclined to believe, a reflection of a more matter-of-fact attitude to council work? One senior Conservative described the approach of some of her fellow Conservatives in the following terms:

I think in my party there is a greater reluctance to accept there is a need for people to do anything other than as a bit of a hobby . . . . (Catherine Thorne, Conservative Chair).

If council work is a hobby, it is something about which careful calculation and forethought is seen to be out of place, inappropriate and unnecessary. These Conservatives are playing the role of the 'well-meaning public-spirited amateur' who sees little need to reflect long on their role, on how to determine policy objectives in an explicit fashion or how to decide in a 'professional' and managerial manner the 'correct strategy' to follow to achieve a particular objective.

Councillors and casework

How significant is casework in the total workload of councillors? In Chapter 3, we suggested there were good grounds for doubting the validity of the workload figures produced by the the Widdicombe investigation. These figures indicated that the typical councillor devotes 13 hours a month (out of a total of 74) to electors' problems, surgeries and pressure groups (Widdicombe 1986c, p. 42). Our own findings (see Figure 3.1, p. 63) show that county councillors spend considerably more time than this: on average, approximately 60 hours per month on 'other activities', a major part of which is casework.

In the Widdicombe postal questionnaire, members were asked to respond to three statements which were closely related to casework. With respect to the first two, there was a very clearcut response with more than 90 per cent agreeing with the first and more than 75 per cent disagreeing with the second:

Elected representatives should represent the views of all the people in their wards, not just those who voted for them.

A councillor has a very busy life and can't give much time to members of the public.

Councillors were deeply divided, however, on the third statement:

People who are aggrieved by maladministration should be able to go directly to the local ombudsman instead of via their local councillor

with approximately equal proportions (40 per cent) agreeing and disagreeing (Widdicombe 1986c, p. 65 and pp. 79–82).

In our experience county councillors have a strongly positive attitude to casework. More than half those we interviewed indicated their acceptance of this aspect of their work, and in contrast, stressed the relative *unimportance* of committee work. We asked what was the most important aspect of the job, and the following comment is typical of many:

> Well, it's certainly not the committee work. The most important aspect is your constituency work, and that's the most rewarding part as well. It's what you actually do for your constituents, that's what they elect you for . . . and that's the most demanding part as well . . . They're interested in their little patch and what they want done . . . You get no allowance for that, in time at all . . . . (Ian Miles, Labour Chair)

We found that Labour councillors were much more likely to comment in positive terms than Conservatives, and Labour and Liberal members also *mentioned* casework more often. Conservatives, on the other hand, hardly talked about casework at all.

How can we explain this imbalance between Labour and Conservative councillors? In this regard it is worth recalling the workload data discussed in Chapter 3. In both the Recall and the Diary, Conservative councillors recorded a lower average number of hours a week on all council and council-related activities. In the Diary, for example, Conservatives recorded a workload more than 20 per cent lighter than Labour members. In Figure 3.3 Councillors' Workloads by Party (p. 64) it is clear that the difference between Conservative and Labour councillors can largely be accounted for in terms of the category 'other activities' (of which casework was a substantial part).

Casework and party differences

Why do Conservative councillors appear to have a lower casework load? One possible explanation is that the areas represented by Conservative members *generate* less casework. Perhaps there is some link between the social and economic character of an area, the inclination of the electorate to vote Conservative and the volume of casework which arises – with poorer areas generating relatively more cases for councillors.

We see some support for this explanation in research carried out for the Widdicombe inquiry. This indicated that people in social class E (casual workers and unemployed) had a 'probability of complaining' which was significantly higher than other social groups. Moreover, it was shown that the alternative channels of complaint (contacting officers, the local MP and the local media) were more likely to be used by owner-occupiers than council tenants, and by social classes AB and C1 than social classes D and E (Widdicombe 1986d, pp. 49–50).

A weakness of this explanation is that it portrays the councillor in reactive or passive terms – as if he or she waits patiently for complaining constituents to turn up – or not turn up as the case may be. Casework, however, as we suggested in Chapter 3, is the main area in which member workload is to some significant extent discretionary, in that the councillor can extend, limit or contract the range of activities undertaken.

This feature of casework – that it is something that can be partly controlled by the councillor – suggests a second possible explanation of party differences in regard to casework. A number of Conservatives said to us, often in the form of incidental comment, that they were more efficient in dealing with casework than councillors in other groups. While the self-justifying nature of such comments is evident, it is possible that the managerial experience of some Conservatives may have given them the necessary skills to deal with these aspects of council work more expeditiously and with fewer disruptive effects to family life. Only the concerned constituent, however, would be able to judge whether such an 'efficient' approach to casework results in the 'effective' solution of problems. We were also aware that in a number of instances, the relatively high managerial status of some Conservatives enabled them unofficially to use their company's secretarial facilities for their public duties.

Not only do councillors regard casework as a very important part of their work but they also see it as their main source of job satisfaction. For more than half of the councillors we spoke to, it was casework where they felt they could have the greatest beneficial effect, as the following comment illustrates.

The things that have given me most satisfaction are not attending meetings or being elected by my political party and being seen to be somebody on some sort of political pedestal . . . and that is if somebody came to me with a problem, I can manage somehow to find my way through the bureaucracy and give somebody some satisfaction ... That I find satisfying. (Maurice Holmes, Conservative backbencher)

It might be expected that backbenchers would be particularly likely to stress their involvement in this aspect of the work. This was not, however, the case. We found that members who were Chairs of committees were just as likely to express this view as backbenchers. Nor was there any apparent difference between female and male councillors.

We also received a substantial number of comments which suggested that some members had a more purposive approach to casework than others. This took a number of forms. Some members stressed that they were always accessible to constituents. For example:

I am a totally committed councillor. Twenty-four hours a day. And that is my password and has been . . . . A problem today will be dealt with today, subject to the officers being available . . . . And it is never left more than twenty-four hours. And I try as often as possible to return a reply to the person within forty-eight hours. (Andrew Moore, Labour backbencher)

Others stressed their 'extra-curricular' casework – the giving of a reference to a constituent applying for work or helping with claims for financial assistance. Several spoke about holding regular surgeries or advice centres to which members of the public could go – probably the most active and planned approach to casework.

Taking all these active approaches together, it was clear to us that Labour members were predominant. Labour councillors are very much more inclined to define their task in terms which demand a proactive and problem-searching role. This is true irrespective of the member's gender, seniority or employment status.

Councillors and the public

Traditionally, a powerful justification for local government (as opposed to regional or national government) rests on the closeness of local councils to voters, charge-payers and consumers of local services. Local councils are uniquely able to detect and respond to the wishes of local people and communities and are best placed to adapt national legislation to meet particular local circumstances.

In the view of councillors, how successful are councils in this regard? The party allegiance of councillors is the major influence here. The Widdicombe postal questionnaire asked members to respond to the following statements:

Too little consultation is held with interested parties before decisions are made.

Ordinary citizens should have more say in the decisions made by local government.

Councillors were evenly divided in their response to the initial statement but there were striking differences between the parties. Conservatives were least enthusiastic (only 31 per cent agreeing) and Liberals were most enthusiastic (66 per cent agreeing) about consulting with interested parties. Local circumstances, however, appear to have influenced the response. Both Labour and Conservative members were unenthusiastic about consultation when their party was in control. Longer-serving councillors also felt less comfortable with the idea of more consultation (Widdicombe 1986c, pp. 73–4).

Almost 60 per cent agreed with the second statement but there were some interesting variations. Councillors from shire districts (51 per cent agreed) and Conservatives (35 per cent agreed) were less enthusiastic about allowing ordinary citizens more say. Seventy-four per cent of Labour and 87 per cent of Liberal members agreed. In contrast to the first statement, councillors' responses were not affected by whether their party was in control or by length of council service (Widdicombe 1986c, p. 75).

It is clear from the Widdicombe interview survey that the role of members as local representatives is taken very seriously. Local knowledge and expertise is likely to be seen as especially relevant in those authorities where there remain significant geographical divisions and strong local community loyalties. In such authorities, officers who are often fairly new to the authority cannot hope to rival members in their knowledge of the local area (Widdicombe 1986b, p. 57).

In talking to county councillors, we found that the largest single group saw themselves as representing their local area or local community. All the Liberal councillors expressed this view – a reflection of the strategy of 'community politics' or highly localised political activity which the Liberal Party has fostered for a number of years.

> of all the councillors at County Hall, whatever I feel about Liberals, they are probably the best community councillors, that's just a little plug for them . . . . I think looking after the interests of people and putting their interests before politics; in other words, let's have people not policies first . . . . (Eleanor Mansfield, Liberal).

This 'community-centred' view was not, however, monopolised by the Liberals, as Conservative and Labour members from all three counties expressed similar views.

In the light of the number of comments we received, women appear to attach greater importance to this facet of a member's duties than men. This was the case irrespective of county, employment or council position. Women also put more emphasis on the need to visit the parishes in the ward and attend parish council meetings.

> on Sunday, my husband and I, we always try to [go] out to a different parish in my ward each weekend . . . . I see it as part of my duty to make sure I just at least *see* the parishes from time to time and keep involved . . . so I do see it as part of my duty . . . . (Marian Gaines, Liberal)

In contrast, a small number of councillors saw themselves as representing the county as a whole rather than any particular part of it.

> Well, I'm put here by people who vote for me and I do a certain amount to try and look after that part – or those whom I represent. That's a fairly simplistic way of putting it because once you get here, you then immediately have to take a wider view. And I always say that it is a luxury that you can't indulge

in too often – to be entirely parochial. (Richard Hall, Conservative Chair)

All such comments came from councillors in one county and most were made by Conservatives (both front- and backbenchers). While many councillors saw themselves as either representing the local community *or* the county as a whole, a substantial minority had a dual allegiance. On the one hand they spoke of 'the people' or 'the voters' in a broad undifferentiated way and, on the other hand, they associated themselves, without any difficulty or sense of conflict, with the county-wide or community-centred view.

We found it remarkable that the strong local loyalties and attachments reflected in these comments had survived in spite of what appeared to be the strictly disciplined political control and a high level of ideological conflict in all three county councils. Certain geographical characteristics may ensure that local loyalties persist. Where, for example, two major urban centres exist within a county, the competition between them for a share of council spending on such faciliies as schools and roads can ensure that many members find that their county-wide party allegiance has to be tempered by more locally-based judgements. Such 'cross-cutting' loyalties also may arise where there is only one major urban centre in a county's area. In such a case the councillors (possibly a minority), representing the suburban or rural hinterland might, in the face of 'domination by the city', wish to assert the interests of their areas at the expense of loyalty to their party group.

Councillors and party control of councils

It has been widely argued that, in the last fifteen years, 'local politics has come to life'; that the local political scene has become more highly charged and that party groups organise and pursue their aims with a ruthlessness which was not commonly found in the 1950s and 1960s (Young and Kramer 1978, Newton 1976, Alexander 1982).

An alternative perspective with a less exclusively contemporary emphasis was the historical survey of party control of local authorities prepared for the Widdicombe Committee. This concluded that party politics in local government was no recent development. Contested elections, for example, predated the creation of the county councils in 1889. Moreover, all political parties have played their part in the development of party control of local authorities (Widdicombe 1986e, Ch. 3).

In our view two interrelated changes have taken place in the last fifteen years. Party politics has become more *intensive* in that the political management of council business by means of group discipline and majority group monopolisation of committee chairs has been followed with greater rigour and determination. Simultaneously, party control has become more *extensive* in that the 'old-style, ostensibly non-partisan politics of the rural areas' has been extinguished. (Gyford *et al.* 1989, p. 26) The party machine has moved out from the city and has colonised surrounding areas.

What do councillors think about party control of local councils? The Widdicombe interview survey found an increasing tendency for those members who were interested in broad policy issues to articulate their interest in party ideological terms; that is, in terms of attaining specific political values and goals. They found, for example, that the more ideological Conservative members had a deep-rooted suspicion of officers' 'empire-building' inclinations which they felt required constant vigilance if local authority spending was to be checked. Comparable suspicions were voiced on the left, where local officials were seen as 'instinctively conservative' and opposed to any socialist change of policy (Widdicombe 1986b, pp. 59–61).

The picture revealed by the postal questionnaire indicates that members' opinions are both less polarised and more complex than this suggests. In the questionnaire, councillors were invited to say whether they agreed or disagreed with the following statement:

The first concern of the elected members of the majority party is to implement the party manifesto.

Overall, a diverse pattern of responses emerged with slightly more than 50 per cent agreeing and 30 per cent disagreeing with the statement. There were, however, major differences in the responses in different kinds of authorities and from different parties. Two-thirds of members from the shire counties, London boroughs and metropolitan authorities agreed with the statement but in the

English shire districts only 44 per cent agreed. Seventy-nine per cent of Labour members agreed but among Liberal and Conservative members, the proportions were 33 per cent and 49 per cent respectively (Widdicombe 1986c, pp. 76–8).

The Widdicombe researchers also asked councillors what changes (if any) had taken place in the role of political parties in their authority over the past few years. Opinions here were also divided, with a third stating there had been no changes and the next largest group – a quarter – pointing to a move to the conduct of council business along party lines (Widdicombe 1986c, p. 79).

We also found a similar diversity of views. Conservatives and minority group members voiced most hostility to party group control of council activities. Amongst those Conservatives who were hostile, however, their discontent was focused on different targets. Some felt that they were hindered in getting things done and that decisions should be taken pragmatically and apolitically, according to 'the merits of the case'.

Frustrations, yes, you get bugger all done . . . It's also . . . that you belong to a political party and my honest opinion . . . would be the fact that I probably think local politics were best when they *were* local politics and there were less politics and . . . more independents and less damn' socialists and damn' Conservatives and grotty Liberals all trying to make their mark on the world. (Jeremy Austin, Conservative backbencher)

Others felt that it was the way in which the party group operated and prevented serious debate which was the major problem.

I try to use group meetings . . . to establish the right course of action, which isn't a success because most people go there having decided on their course of action and they object to their course of action being questioned . . . . (Paul Jackson, Conservative backbencher)

We initially expected that this antipathy towards the party group would be most evident among those who had first served on councils as independents when party politics was less pervasive. This was not, however, the case. While half of the councillors who made this kind of comment had been first elected in the 1960s and 1970s, the other half had been elected more recently.

A smaller number of minority group members (of all parties) complained of the way in which the party system rendered them impotent as far as the making of policy was concerned.

I suppose the disappointment comes with being in opposition and . . . very often losing and not being able to get what you want – what the public needs. Especially if it's something you think they really need to carry on life, and you're very disappointed . . . I don't feel I've been as effective as I could have been in power . . . . The only thing you can do in opposition is to keep on plugging. (Brenda Lyall, Labour backbencher)

More positive views were expressed by a rather larger number of councillors drawn equally from the Labour and Conservative parties. All emphasised the need to support party policy.

I'm a very firm believer in the group system and in group discipline. I do feel very strongly that if you have that the group is the place to have disagreements about policy and to state your case. If you can't get everybody else to agree with your point of view then I would abide by the group's decision . . . . (Carol Stothard, Conservative backbencher)

Taken together, negative and positive views were expressed by members from all parties. Conservative attitudes to the party system, however, seem more diverse or contradictory than Labour attitudes. Some Conservatives are clearly disinclined to accept wholeheartedly the present-day politically-controlled local authorities. On the other hand, rather more Conservatives are prepared 'to play the game' with as much care and relish as their Labour or Liberal opponents.

Councillors and officers

In addition to the regular formal meetings of the council and its committees, members and (mainly) senior officers meet in working groups, on site visits and trips to conferences and in other more informal settings. Until very recently little was known about the nature of officer–councillor relationships which develop from these contacts. One reviewer of earlier research described the relationship as 'largely unexplained at present' (Gyford 1984, p. 3). Another said that studying the relationship is 'like trying to get blood out of red tape' (Newton 1976, p 146). A third said that it had proved impossible 'to break through the cultural cliché that [the officer] was simply the servant advising the all-powerful policymaking councillors whose decisions they readily implemented' (Dearlove 1973, p. 229).

In a similar vein, though with considerable understatement, the Widdicombe Report said:

> We must accept that the current local government model, for all its strengths, is not one which lends itself to total clarity in roles and relationships. (Widdicombe 1986a, p. 103)

The research carried out for the Widdicombe inquiry has thrown some light on councillors' views on member–officer relations. The overall impression gained by the researchers was one of satisfaction; most members talked in positive terms about the relations which operated in their authorities. Any discussion of friction and difficulties, say the authors of the research, should therefore be seen in the context of a generally positive evaluation.

Somewhat paradoxically, however, the researchers then detailed a number of major aspects of the member–officer relationship where there had been an increase in tension and conflict. These aspects included, for example, the setting of agendas for committee meetings, the drafting and redrafting of committee reports and the appointment of officers. In these (and other) respects, many members were increasingly assertive and were attempting, not always successfully, to realign the traditional boundary between themselves and officers (Widdicombe 1986b, Ch. 6).

Discontent with member–officer relations is further reflected in the postal questionnaire which asked councillors to respond to the following statement:

> Council officials have too much influence on decision-making.

Overall, almost half of the councillors agreed that council officials had too much influence, with one-third disagreeing. On this issue, in contrast to those we have discussed earlier, differences between councillors in different types of authority and from different parties were not great. More significant in shaping attitudes were local circumstances. Recently-elected councillors were more inclined to agree with the statement than councillors who had ten or more years of service – a possible confirmation of the widespread impression that the new generation of members are more assertive (or less well socialised or informed?) than their predecessors. Minority group members were more inclined to agree with the statement than majority group members – irrespective of whether they were Labour or Conservative. Those who had the greatest direct contact with officers, for example, committee Chairs, were only slightly less inclined to agree (45 per cent) than were those members who held no office (51 per cent) (Widdicombe 1986c, pp. 66–9).

Of the county councillors we spoke to, one third made some kind of comment on their relationships with officers. Members' opinions were more diverse than one would expect in the light of the Widdicombe data. The positive comments stressed the 'expert' or 'executive' nature of the officer's job, the value of cooperative working and the need to listen to the advice which officers gave.

> I would say, deal with officers with respect because they are experts. You are the person that formulates the policies but the officers are your experts and your dictionary, your fund of information, and I've always found them first class, first class . . . . (Herbert Jeffreys, Conservative backbencher)

An equal number of negative comments suggested that the member should be a watchdog prepared to challenge or 'catch out' the officer. The public should be protected against their influence and activities.

> I make a point of talking to officers when they are least expecting me to . . . . I turn up out of the blue and never at the same time twice . . . with officers [department named]. I've

always gone straight into their department when I have a problem, and I've always caught them out up to now, because they're the laziest, lousiest department on the council . . . . (Gary Coulson, Labour Chair)

Other comments in a similar vein implied that officers were too powerful, that there was a need to keep your distance and that officers intimidated new councillors.

We received as many negative as positive comments. The positive comments were made by councillors irrespective of their party, gender and council position. The negative comments, however, came disproportionately from members who held committee chairs. This was true regardless of party, gender and county and does not corroborate the findings of the Widdicombe research (with respect to the views of office-holders) to which we referred earlier. We did not expect (and did not receive) any comments which suggested that officers were seen in the traditionally stereotypical terms as deferential servants of the council. Nonetheless, we feel it remarkable that those councillors who had had the greatest day-to-day contact with officers commonly expressed various shades of hostility towards them.

Council work: a full-time commitment or a part-time leisure activity?

In Chapter 3, we argued that councillors' workloads are very much higher than has been officially recognised; and that the number of hours devoted to council-related work varies according to gender, party, and council position. But do many members see their duties as a full-time job or not? What are the general attitudes of councillors to the work they do? How far do they feel free to define their roles?

A rough definition of a full-time councillor would be a member who spends 35 to 40 hours a week on council work. The proportion of members who could be classed as full-timers is difficult to determine. The very impressionistic evidence from the Widdicombe interviews implies a cautious conclusion. This suggests that in 50 per cent of the authorities which were visited there were no full-time members; in 20 per cent there were 'one or two' and in the remaining 30 per cent there were more than 'one or two' (Widdicombe 1986b, p. 66).

Unfortunately data on councillors' workhours in various official inquiries have been presented as averages and it is, therefore, impossible to determine with accuracy the proportion of members whose hours of work were considerably in excess of the average. Nonetheless, the fact that more than two decades ago, councillors on county borough councils were, on *average*, spending almost 20 hours a week on council business suggests that there was at that time a significant minority of members in the larger urban areas willing to devote themselves to council work on a full-time basis (Maud 1967b, p. 93).

We draw a similar conclusion from the information from the Widdicombe postal questionnaire (which, as we said in Chapter 3, tends to understate members' workloads). Councillors in Scottish region and island councils spent more than 32 hours and those in the Welsh counties more than 27 hours on council duties in an average week. In these authorities, we feel that it is highly likely that there is a substantial proportion of members who are working a full week.

The information we received from county councillors also provides a partial answer to the second part of the question. As we explained in Chapter 3, we had Diary data from 55 councillors and 21 recorded approximately 40 hours or more in the 'Diary' week. Of these 21, 15 were Labour members, 14 were committee chairs or group leaders and 12 were female.

The conclusion we draw from the evidence is that there is a significant proportion of elected members who spend the equivalent to a full working week on their council activities; that these 'full-timers' are more likely to be found in both the more urbanised and the more geographically extensive authorities; and that they are more likely to be Labour members in senior positions.

We are surprised that such a substantial minority exists in the face of sustained official discouragement. In Chapter 6, we discussed the operation of the system of attendance allowances and argued that it works against those councillors who define their council work as a full-time commitment. Moreover, the views of successive governments and committees of inquiry have largely been hostile to the idea of the full-time member. Both the Robinson and Widdicombe Committees were apprehensive about the effect on officer–member relations and on relations with the public. The Widdicombe Report commented that the full-time member would want to intervene in the day-to-day administration of services. This would create a twofold danger:

> First, there is a danger that chief officers will see their management responsibilities undermined, that they will become demoralised and that this will be reflected in rapid staff turnover (of which there is some evidence). Second, there is a danger that it will alter the character of councillors so that they will become full-time administrators rather than people who are representative of the local community which they serve. (Widdicombe 1986a, p. 127)

The Conservative government broadly endorsed this point of view and argued that

> local government officers should re-establish their position of independence . . . . I don't think they can do that if they have sitting on their shoulders political masters who are involved in every decision. They need independence from that. (Local Government Minister John Gummer in *Local Government Chronicle*, 3 February 1989)

Approximately one in three council members we spoke to referred to their work as a full-time commitment. Most of these were women. Some stressed the unintended way in which their duties had grown and reflected on the implications as they saw them.

> I would say that I've almost become a full-time councillor, not by choice but by the evolution of time really . . . . I don't want a full-time job in local politics . . . but that's virtually what it is now . . . . (Catherine Thorne, Conservative Chair)

Others emphasised the way in which the work is very demanding and can become totally absorbing.

I mean if I was dithering about with it – like dipping your toe
into the water instead of jumping in and getting involved with
things. And sorting things out that want sorting out instead of
skirting around the edges of it and just fiddling with it and
leaving it to the officers to deal with . . . . (Lillian Tutt, Liberal)

As we saw in Chapter 6, some went further and saw the need for a
salary.

I actually think now – I didn't think when I became a councillor
– [I] actually think that the big authorities like a county council,
metropolitan and big districts, that there should be some
provision for you actually to do it as a full-time job, where
you can claim a wage a bit like maternity leave – there's a central
fund and your employer can claim from that central fund . . . .
(Sarah Hibbert, Labour backbencher)

In addition to those members who expressed a 'full-time' view,
there were a number of councillors whose sentiments of 'total
commitment' (reflected in the following montage) were very similar
but showed a very strong sense of vocation.

to get yourself involved in the community . . . be available at all
times . . . you have to be prepared to give up leisure time and
interests and things that you do . . . . I always did my best for
them . . . . I would always find out . . . I mean, people have
problems and we have them in here [front room] privately I
maintain if you're a councillor, you've got to *be* a councillor and
that has been my life . . . to work for people. (Various
councillors)

In contrast to those who saw council work either as a full-time
job (in terms of hours) or as requiring total commitment (in that it
is the member's dominant life interest), a small number of
councillors saw their role and the degree of commitment required
in more limited terms. Some suggested that being a councillor was
(and should remain) a partial commitment and questioned the
motivations of some members who appeared to inflate artificially
the demands of the job. Others saw dangers in councils not being
able to draw upon outside experience.

A lot of people make more or less of the job of being a councillor to suit their own feelings. I think they should perhaps be a little more honest with themselves . . . . (Clive Stephens, Conservative backbencher)

I think you've got to have a cross section of people on the council . . . . I think you need different people to fulfil different roles . . . and if you're too centrally council-orientated, then you don't give the council any experience from elsewhere. (Carol Stothard, Conservative backbencher)

Some male councillors, mostly Conservative, saw their council work as a leisure activity or hobby.

I take [the county council] as being, if you can say it . . . it's a leisure activity, learning more about the county . . . just enjoying life, that's it. (Herbert Jeffreys, Conservative backbencher)

Some members attempted a 'normal business hours' approach which limited council activities to certain days or times of the week.

Well, from about 5 o'clock we are really pretty free . . . My husband has always been very against endless evening meetings and he has tried to avoid them, because there are councillors we know who are out every evening to various meetings and he's always really thought it was a bit unnecessary. (Mrs Rivendell, wife of Conservative Chair)

While these councillors attempted to delimit their tasks in terms of time, others, all Labour members, argued that it was not possible (and not desirable) to define the boundaries of their role because many members of the public did not distinguish between the functions of county and district councils.

For one thing, most people don't know the difference between a district councillor and a county councillor. They still bring all their housing problems to me and I have to fetch the borough councillor . . . but then again, if people have tried elsewhere and can't get anywhere, somebody's got to try and push for them. (Barbara Morgan, Labour Chair)

How councillors define their role in these general terms, and whether or not they wish to and are able to put limits on what they do, appears to reflect distinctions of party, council position and to some extent gender. Male Conservative backbenchers limit their activities either because they interpret the role as one that makes no great demands on them, or because they view council activity as another form of leisure. Labour members appear much less likely to view their role in those ways and often take on duties which lie outside a strict legal definition of their responsibilities.

What county councillors did not say

As we will explain in the Appendix, the interviews with county councillors produced a very large amount of information, only part of which has been used in this book. Councillors (and their partners) usually spoke at great length about council work, family affairs and employment and we believe that the length of the interviews and the quality of the information we received are indications of the rapport we established. Given these circumstances, we feel we should comment on what councillors did not say in spite of the opportunities which we provided.

Previous research led us to expect, for example, that councillors holding senior positions would express a significantly different set of attitudes about their roles. In fact, as we have remarked above, this 'seniority' influence appeared to be relatively weak. They had, on average, a heavier workload than backbenchers, but were not differentiated in many other ways from the other county councillors to whom we spoke.

In other respects, councillors did not respond in the ways previous studies led us to expect. Much has been written about the representational roles of elected members with some being 'trustees' (which entails the exercise of the member's own judgement of what is correct or just) and some being delegates (which involves the members accepting a mandate from the party or pressure group). None of the councillors appeared aware of this dichotomy, but many seemed to combine both aspects in different measure in a pragmatic fashion.

Recently, some writers have observed that there is a recognisable trend to the production of more detailed local election manifestos, whose clear purpose is to guide council policymaking once power has been won at the ballot box. (Gyford *et al.* 1989, p. 167; Widdicombe 1986b, p. 92). All the councillors we spoke to had been elected as party candidates, but their party's policies or manifesto seemed to intrude only occasionally into their deliberations. This was true even for those members who seemed most oriented towards policymaking. We are not suggesting that partisan decisions were not made. Clearly they were, in all three counties. But party policy, whether national or local, is commonly framed at such a level of generality that members *in committee* have considerable discretion over timing, funding, the allocation of schemes to particular areas of the county and over how to respond to such major and unpredictable matters as changes in the size of the authority's revenue support grant.

We further expected that some councillors would express views which would reflect the 'elite domination' of their authority. Theories of elite domination – where councils are run by an informal and unaccountable clique comprising senior members and officers – have been the stock-in-trade of much academic comment for many years. We have noted earlier that many councillors were critical of officers and it is possible that these sentiments were a manifestation of resentment against the way their authority was being run. We feel, however, that if the domination of their authority had been seen by members as oppressive we would have received many critical comments about political leadership either of the council as a whole or the party group. The silence of members in this regard is an eloquent statement of either their fatalism, or at best, their broad satisfaction at the way matters are handled in their council. We are strongly inclined to the view that theories of elite domination reflect a 'top-down' perspective of the local authority and overlook or understate the extent to which councillors both in committees and as caseworkers are able to exercise considerable discretion and to play a meaningful and satisfying role.

The relationship of councillors to pressure groups is subject to much contemporary comment and is another area where responses did not match our original preconceptions. The Widdicombe Report commented that society is becoming increasingly sectionalised, with interest groups such as ratepayers, farmers' groups and racial and sexual minorities having a direct input into local government, bypassing elected members. Moreover, sectional interests bring pressure to bear on councillors who find it more difficult to adopt a balanced relationship with the local community. In its extreme form, the position of the councillor is reduced to that of a delegate (Widdicombe 1986a, pp. 104–5).

We find it difficult to imagine that councillors would be ignorant or unaware of these pressures and believe that in the context of several hours of confidential open-ended discussion they would have expressed any strong feelings they had in this regard. In the event, very few members voiced any concern or claimed that they represented sectional interests. Pressure groups which were very local in operation – that is, limited to a councillor's division or local parish – seemed to evoke a clear-cut (and generally cooperative) response and members were prepared to champion their case in spite of some occasional misgivings. This activity came very close to the casework that most councillors accepted (with varying degrees of enthusiasm).

The picture we have, therefore, is not one of councillors clearly choosing whether they should be a trustee or a delegate. Neither is it one of members being unduly preoccupied with external pressures from party or sectional interests or resentful that political power was in the hands of a few. We would emphasise the extent to which councillors, both individually and collectively, have a large measure of autonomy. Advice from officers, party group unity and community support also enable members to deal as selectively with the external world as they think fit.

Three kinds of councillor

We found major differences between councillors in how they define their role. We can divide these differences along two contrasting dimensions: party allegiance and gender.

As we have seen, party allegiance is closely related to the emphasis which the councillor chooses to place on different aspects of the member's role. Labour members saw their council work as a *job* and were concerned to specialise in particular aspects of their work. They spoke more readily about the need to make policy decisions, had a more active approach to casework and were less inclined to put clear limits on their role.

In contrast, Conservatives, while endorsing the general importance of casework, were much less preoccupied with it than Labour members. They were much more sceptical about consulting with the public (and interest groups) and particularly stressed conscientious attendance at council and committee meetings. They had more diverse (or conflicting) views than Labour councillors on representation (many expressing a dual allegiance to ward and county), on party politics and on the issue of full-time councillors. In brief, Conservatives exhibited a much wider range of attitudes – from the traditional 'amateur' conception of the role to that of the 'full-time professional' – than did either Labour or Liberal members. The most distinctive feature of Liberal attitudes was the emphasis placed on 'community politics' – but even here both Labour and Conservatives would stake claims.

We also found significant differences of emphasis between how male and female councillors defined their role. Women more frequently expressed a 'community-centred' view of their duties as elected representatives, and laid greater stress on the need for attendance at parish and community council meetings. Most significantly, they were much readier to see their council work as a full-time activity. In essence, irrespective of party and council position, female members expressed a view of the councillor's role which required a degree of commitment and consistency comparable to that required of someone working in a professional capacity. This greater commitment was reflected in their work-hours.

Council position appeared to be a much weaker influence on how members see their roles than either party or gender. Senior councillors had more regular contact with officers (compared to backbenchers) but this had not resulted in a more positive view of member–officer relations. There was a somewhat greater readiness among senior councillors, as opposed to backbenchers, to see themselves as 'full-timers'. When we examined this difference more closely, however, it was evident only in the case of male Conservatives. We therefore believe that the main factors influencing the perceptions of the 'full-timer' are party and gender rather than council position.

In the light of our research, we have identified two divergent approaches which we believe may be applied to all councillors. On the one hand, there are those who have a limited or 'minimalist' view of the councillor's role. Typically, such people emphasise attendance at council and committee meetings and undertake all the preparation they consider necessary. They attract very little casework, and when cases do arise they can usually deal with them quickly at a time convenient to themselves and their families.

At the other extreme are the councillors who take a 'proactive' stance to their work. Although they attend council and committee meetings regularly, they regard this as one of the least important aspects of their work, except in those cases when they can, as a result of their position on a particular committee, play a crucial role in determining policy. Typically, they believe they are on the council to 'provide a service to the community'. They fulfil that commitment by making themselves available at all times, by publicising their availability and by keeping themselves informed about the problems of their areas. They will, therefore, take part in such activities as attending parish council meetings, holding surgeries, visiting outlying suburbs and villages regularly, putting out ward newsletters and generally taking a very active part in local affairs.

Within this proactive group, there are two alternative approaches. Some councillors regard their work as a vocation. Their public and private worlds are virtually identical. There is no interference with their private life because the council is their life. They have no other activity – neither employment nor leisure. This contrasts with the minimalists, for whom council work is also a leisure activity, but one which they strictly control.

For neither of these groups is council work a problem; however, the impact on their families varies greatly. We found in Part III that whereas the partners of the minimalists experienced little disruption, the partners and other family members of those who saw council work as a vocation were – willingly or otherwise – drawn into the councillor's public world themselves. Depending on their attitude, this could either enrich their own lives, or result in discord and even the breakdown of family relationships.

Other councillors, in contrast to both these groups, take the view that council work is or should be a full-time job. Whereas the vocationalists do not expect or need to earn money from their council work (though preferring not to lose it either), those who see their public duties as a 'job' believe that their full-time or near full-time commitment should be rewarded financially. It is these members who experience most difficulty in reconciling the conflicting demands of their public and private lives. This was the case particularly if they already had other work – as an employee or a parent of a young family – and were unable either to give up those responsibilities or to delegate them to others. Even if they had few other duties, however, their lives were not completely free from problems. Their inability to take on paid employment was of great concern to them and many of them needed, or would have liked, a regular income – something the job of councillor was unlikely to offer them. Partners, too, were often obliged to help the councillor – sometimes in a 'personal assistant' capacity – and this could lead to resentment, which, if not resolved, could disrupt family relationships.

The categories we have put forward relate to attitudes and expectations rather than to the actual hours devoted to council work – though there was a correlation between how the councillor defined the role and the workhours recorded. Unsurprisingly, those who believed that members should always be available and that they should go out looking for problems rather than simply waiting passively for them to be brought to their attention did spend more hours on council work than those who believed their overriding commitment was to meetings of the council and its committees and who reacted to, rather than searched out, constituency complaints.

We wish to emphasis that these categories should be seen as ideal types; no councillor conformed completely to all the criteria of one or other model. In the following three brief biographies, we illustrate both these different councillor styles and the unique qualities of each councillor.

George Peters: council work as a hobby

Mr Peters, a Conservative backbench councillor on a Labour-controlled council in his first term, is a self-employed architect, married with two pre-school children. He became involved in council work because he 'wanted to do something' and 'had a wish to influence events'. Before he became a county councillor, he had stood for the district council, but failed to get elected. He still sees his interest as primarily at the district level because he is debarred by his occupation from membership of those county council committees in which he is most interested.

Mr Peters says that his wife was 'forewarned' that he wished to become a councillor as he had already stood for the district before he met her. She was a Conservative Party member before her marriage and has been quite happy to hold fundraising events at their very large house as this sort of political activity was customary in her family.

Compared to some councillors, Mr Peters leads a very unpressured life. He has a very small workload and averages three or four committee meetings a month. His other public commitments – as a JP and a governor for two schools – take very little time. Because he normally knows well in advance when meetings will take place, and can control his own working hours, he ensures that he does not make appointments that will clash. He does not find paperwork a problem, reads fast and can 'distinguish subject matter from verbiage' without difficulty.

He feels his business is affected by his council commitments as he cannot be given commissions by the county council and, being the only professionally qualified person in his firm, loses business when he is not at work. But he is not too concerned because this has not become a serious problem. The effects on Mr Peters' family life have been very limited. He says that he would not have got involved if it had required constant evening meetings; but the occasional evening commitment is no hardship. Household work is divided strictly on lines of gender.

Mrs Peters is a very supportive wife who says, for example,

> If he's going to do it, he'll do it, so all I can do is to make the path a little easier.

She was brought up in a Conservative family and she takes her Conservatism for granted. Her interests are home-centred and she remarks that her husband's council work has had very little impact on her life. He would, she said, have been out of the house all day in any case. She takes a few telephone calls for him but these are not serious interruptions.

Overall, this is a household that takes voluntary involvement very much for granted, and has not found the demands of council work any greater than any other leisure-time activity.

Robert Paulton: council work as a vocation

Mr Paulton is a Chair of a major committee in a Conservative-controlled authority. He is married with adult children and is self-employed. He says he is very prominent in a number of national organisations connected with local government and showed us his two-page *curriculum vitae* which listed his membership of a large number of national bodies. He seems to fill all his commitments extremely conscientiously and describes himself as 'a dedicated councillor' and says that 'pressures never bother him'.

Mr Paulton started his political career as an independent councillor on a rural district council in the 1950s and his commitment has grown steadily since then. He is currently on the district and parish council as well as the county council. He stresses that this level of commitment is possible only because he is self-employed and because his son now helps to run the business:

> so that his father can fool about at County Hall . . . I'm unemployable because if I went along to a company . . . they'd say, thank you very much Mr Paulton, but we can get somebody who works *here* five days a week, not work at County Hall five days a week.

He sees casework as an important if irritating part of council work but says that he gets quite a lot of it because 'I'm known to pick them up', whereas many members in his position discourage such contact with electors. He finds the slow working of bureaucracy somewhat frustrating and derives great pleasure from taking officers to task for slowness and incompetence. The satisfactions he gets from his work are fighting for his electors – which he sees as most important-and contributing to the running of the community. To this end, he strives to avoid any hint of bribery by having very little social life – he feels that some people would only pretend to be friendly in order to be granted planning permission or some other such favour – 'I've got a very strict code . . .'.

Mr Paulton seems to hold his wife in high regard – 'a very dedicated wife'. He recognises that he could not do all the things he does if his wife did not take care of the domestic side of things and help with the business as well. He says that being a councillor might occasionally be difficult for her when she is left overnight but 'she's too kind to complain'. In his view, she is a very quiet and unassuming person who has only gradually become involved in the local community.

Mrs Paulton was in some ways a surprise. She is extremely supportive but she is not as unassuming as Mr Paulton suggested. She admitted to some complaints and irritation in the early years but now, she says, she has more patience and sees that her husband needs the stimulus of public life. She is critical of the Conservative Party and the 'snobby' attitudes of some Conservatives and says that she voted for a different party in one national election.

Both Mr Paulton and his wife dislike the 'political' tendency of local councils – by which they mean *party* politics. He finds it irritating that no matter how effective his speech may be, in the end the majority vote according to the party line. In brief, Mr Paulton is a very heavily-committed councillor but, because he enjoys what he does, he experiences no pressure, and his family support him both domestically and in his business in order to allow him to do what he wants to do.

Janice Painter: council work as a job

Janice Painter holds a committee Chair in a Labour-controlled authority. She is not employed and is married with young children. She and her husband are both very active in the Labour Party and have held offices at ward and constituency level. Mr Painter is also an active trade unionist and Mrs Painter has been involved in the women's sections of the Labour Party for some years. She sees her duties as a councillor as a natural progression from these earlier activities.

Mrs Painter has two young daughters – one under school age – and as a result has no paid employment. Her husband works shifts as a maintenance engineer, and is, therefore, able to help with child-care, but otherwise she pays a childminder. Without her husband's help, the disruptive effects of council work would be unacceptable. Although she had a good idea of the work involved before she stood for election, she had not expected that she would have so many meetings to attend or things to do, nor had she anticipated taking on the Chair of a committee within a few weeks of first being elected. She comments that the Labour group on the council and senior officers have been very helpful and supportive. She has found her work as a councillor very satisfying, particularly her work on the committee of which she is the Chair where she has been instrumental in pushing certain policies through the Labour group, and then through the Council. She thinks, however, it is very frustrating that the Council is not doing enough: there are so many issues and not enough time to tackle them effectively.

Mrs Painter feels that becoming a councillor has had effects on her casual social contacts around her area. She is just not around to chat to people any more. Moreover, time with her husband is in short supply. Whereas before, when her husband was at home in the day, they could have gone out together or she would have stayed in with the children, now that is no longer possible. Neither of them, however, seem at all resentful or concerned about this, but take it for granted as a consequence of the choices they have jointly taken. Both of them are conscious, however, of the need to plan time very carefully, rather than doing things casually as it occurs to them to do them. She says council work is never finished and that it's always in her mind. They go out very little and feel that their social life is very much tied up with the Labour Party. Mr Painter sees his political activities and trade union activities as complementary to those of his wife.

This is very much a political household: politics is the main interest of both of them and political discussion is such a constant part of their life together that, as Mrs Painter says, it is impossible to separate the political parts of the day from the non-political. This shared commitment makes possible the inconvenience and limitations which council work imposes on the family.

Conclusion: councillors' roles, attitudes and expectations

Underlying the unique characteristics of each elected member are general and recurrent patterns which show the links between party, the definition of role, family, employment and gender. We present these patterns schematically in Table 7.1 overleaf.

This table indicates both diversity and difference: councillors, in general, may define their work as they think fit. We applaud this diversity but think that Parliament, the political parties and local authorities unnecessarily discourage and limit those members who

TABLE 7.1   Political styles

	Council activity as		
	Hobby	*Vocation*	*Job*
Can one make a distinction between the public/private?	Yes	No	Yes
Can the boundary between public and private be maintained in practice?	Yes	No	No
Involvement of partner and/or family	Low	High	High
Is this a 'political household'?	No	No	Probably
Approach to casework	Reactive	Proactive	Proactive
Workhours in relation to average	Lower	Higher	Higher
Should members be paid?	No	No	Yes
Typical gender, party allegiance and council position	Male Conservative backbenchers	Female/Male Conservative Chairs & female backbenchers, all parties	Female & male Labour Chairs & male Labour backbenchers

see their council duties in more expansive terms. This denial of *greater* diversity has the effect, if not the intention, of loading the dice, so to speak, against many councillors and reflects the failure of Parliament and successive governments to recognise the growing complexity of local government and of popular participation in local political activity. In the final chapter we consider what can be done to foster a much greater diversity of involvement by elected members in the government of the local community.

8 Conclusion: What Can be Done?

Introduction

We have argued throughout this book that local government faces a crisis. At the centre of this crisis, though largely disregarded in the contemporary debate, is the councillor. He or she is faced with many conflicting demands: from fellow councillors, from officers, from political parties, from the public and from central government. At the same time, since council work is essentially a voluntary unpaid activity, most members cannot devote as much time to it as they feel it requires, but must balance their public demands against those coming from the more private sphere of life. Employers, spouses and children are foremost here. Nor must the need for adequate leisure time be forgotten: though, to some, their council duties are a leisure activity, most regard them – understandably – as work, and hope for at least some time to themselves, free from other demands, so that they can return refreshed to the tasks that face them.

In this book, we have summarised all the evidence we could find that has a bearing on the home and working lives of local politicians. Inevitably, we have had to rely heavily on our own work, which, in its focus on the interface between public and private responsibilities, has few precedents. We find it surprising that there has been so little official and academic interest in how – or whether – councillors cope with the job, and virtually no concern for their welfare.

At this point we will summarise the main findings of our research, and then go on to consider some of the possible future developments in local government. We will then look briefly at the situation in other countries. We will consider how some of the worst problems facing members can be alleviated and will end with a brief list of recommendations which we hope will influence the course of the debate on the future of local government.

Summary of findings

Workloads

The central finding, which underpins our analysis, concerns the size and nature of councillors' workloads. The council members we talked to spent on average thirty-five hours per week on their council work and other related activities; that is, the equivalent of a full-time job. Some of the most highly-committed members spent sixty hours or more in busy weeks; though, to balance that, we spoke to one or two councillors who managed to limit their commitments to two or three hours.

Why are our figures at so much variance with those from other studies? As we pointed out in Chapter 3, the official inquiries undertaken by the Maud, Robinson and Widdicombe Committees had three major weaknesses. First, in order to maximise their sample size at minimum cost, they used postal questionnaires, which do not allow for the meticulous probing and careful questioning that we, in our face-to-face interviews, supplemented by self-completion Diaries, were able to employ.

Secondly, in asking about a 'typical week', previous researchers were encouraging councillors to make estimates of a kind which, almost inevitably, would ignore passing conversations, interruptions, phone calls and even the reading of council papers, which most members experience on a more or less daily basis. Thirdly, some kinds of 'informal' work, and some political party activities, were deliberately left out of their investigations.

Council workloads are not only twice as large as others have suggested, but the *nature* of the work is rather different from what those who focus on 'approved duties' might have expected. We found that the members with the highest council workloads were also those who spent most time on casework with members of the public, and on preparation for council meetings. This kind of work is often done from home, in odd moments and 'free' time (evenings and weekends). It is often hard to quantify, and cannot be programmed or anticipated, but for these reasons, can be especially intrusive. Our data show that a minority of members were able to control these kinds of interruptions quite stringently, but that the majority accepted them, albeit reluctantly in some cases.

Ways of coping

When we looked at councillors' coping strategies, we could identify three persistent patterns or 'role types'. The first type treated council work as a hobby, and managed to keep it to a part-time leisure activity. Members who favoured this approach tended to be male and Conservative, in full-time employment, and able to be quite ruthless in controlling the external demands that were made of them.

Secondly, there were those who regarded their council work as a vocation. Most of them had no other employment and were able to devote themselves full-time to the task, often bringing their families in as well. Men who favoured this pattern tended to be retired, whereas women would be married with adult children (or none at all) and with a partner who could support them (and was happy to do so) comfortably.

Finally, there were those who, while giving an equivalent time to their public commitments, preferred to regard their council work as a job for which – unfortunately – they were not paid, but should be. Because they saw it as a job, they tried to maintain clear boundaries between their public life and their private leisure and family time – often with limited success. Most of these councillors were relatively young (under 45) and had young families, and, often, career aspirations that were being sacrificed while they devoted themselves full-time to their political and community activities.

When a council member was married, the kind and degree of support offered by the partner was often crucial in allowing them to continue with their public roles, We found that – whatever their misgivings – both husbands and wives usually gave some, and often considerable, support to their activist spouses. The support of husbands was, however, almost always limited and conditional. Where the wife was the activist and where both husband and wife agreed on the importance of the political goals she was fighting for, he was often prepared to back her up by taking some of the work of running the home off her shoulders. These were the 'political households' we described in Chapters 4 and 5. On the other hand, if he had more reservations about the value of her political commitment, he would often help grudgingly, or not at all.

In contrast, wives – whether or not they agreed with their husbands' political ideals – would unquestioningly keep the home running smoothly, and therefore make it possible for men to devote themselves single-mindedly to their public lives. We found that even the least supportive wives – who complained frequently – were nonetheless providing more in the way of *practical* support than even the most impressive of husbands. This means that, for women who want to undertake this work,the task will inevitably be much harder than for men. The imbalance between female and male recruitment is therefore only to be expected: moreover, it is surprising that women are coming forward as often as they are.

Who would be a councillor?

So – given all the difficulties and pressures – why do people come forward at all for election to local councils? Part of the answer is that they don't: very few individuals volunteer to become council candidates. Most were pushed into it. The pool from which candidates may be selected is potentially quite wide. It includes the membership of political parties, but it can also encompass others who are involved in the community in various ways. Council candidates do not have to represent a political party – though most of them now do – but even some of those who are politically identified as Conservatives or Liberal Democrats have no formal party affiliation, or else their membership is of very recent date. In investigating the question of recruitment, we therefore drew a sample from various sources, to include political and community activists of various kinds, and first-time candidates.

Among candidates, we found that the vast majority had drifted into it, usually as a result of party pressure from colleagues, close friends or acquaintances. Most of them felt some sense of moral obligation or duty to help their party or the community, in the absence of alternative candidates. A minority were, however, 'intenders' in the sense that they had a longstanding ambition to run for the council, and thereby to play a part in local decision-making. It is this small group, only, whose route to the council chamber can be adequately explained by the conventional model of the recruitment process.

Of the non-candidates, a high proportion had effectively resisted the pressure from colleagues and others and had remained firm in their wish *not* to extend their political and community activities as far as council membership. Some of them felt quite strongly that they did not have the personal capacity to undertake the work. Some also recognised that the multiple and conflicting demands from their families and employment would, at this stage of their lives, prove too much for them.

So what can be done to encourage more people to come forward for council work, and to make the task easier for them once they are there? How can we encourage the recruitment of younger people, women and ethnic minorities, people with young families or in full-time employment? How can we ensure that – if such individuals do come forward in greater numbers to take up this challenge – neither they nor their families will suffer, personally or financially, from the choice they have made? We will defer consideration of these questions until after we have looked at the international scene and have assessed the likely development of local government in the future.

International comparisons

The value and relevance of the experience of other countries is always open to dispute because the local government systems of the western democracies vary in many ways. Important differences exist in the range of functions and powers allocated to local councils, the discretion with which those functions are exercised and the degree of influence that local authorities can bring to bear on other levels of government (Widdicombe 1986e, p. 157). Comparisons with other countries can, however, illuminate those particular ways in which the scale and practice of British local government are significantly different from other countries. As Norton has said:

> We may be able to breed sturdier hybrids through some of the cross-fertilisations that cross-national reviews suggest, as well as gain such wisdom about our own system as is available only through seeing it in relation to others. (Norton 1985, para. 2)

Two reviews of the broad political and constitutional context of different local government systems show the deviant position of British local authorities. A Council of Europe report covering fourteen countries in Europe refers to a strong movement towards decentralised services and to the transfer of powers from central governments to local and regional authorities (Council of Europe 1981, pp. 12–13). In a more recent study Norton examined local authorities in seven western democracies and commented that in no other country has there been the trend to centralisation of services that has occurred in Britain since the war (Norton 1985, para. 108).

The size of councils in Britain is another distinctive feature of British local government. The typical British local authority has approximately fifty elected members (Widdicombe 1986a, p. 24), whereas most foreign local authorities are half this size or less (Widdicombe 1986e, pp. 140–1). Furthermore, as Table 8.1 shows, local authorities in England and Wales serve very much larger populations than in most other western democracies.

TABLE 8.1   Average population size of local authorities

England and Wales	122 740
Sweden	29 527
Denmark	17 963
Australia	14 125
USA	12 000
Norway	8 891
New Zealand	7 980
Italy	6 717
Canada	5 011
West Germany	2 694
France	1 320

Source: Widdicombe 1986e, p. 140, Table 5.4.

In this regard we endorse the conclusions of the Widdicombe researchers that the size of local authorities in Britain has a direct effect on the working life of council members. It has implications for the hours they put in, for the numbers of committees and sub-committees on which they sit, and for the extent to which they specialise in particular areas of council work (Widdicombe 1986e, p. 141).

The large populations served by British local authorities have an important consequence in that the ratio of council members to citizens is very high. In England and Wales there is approximately one councillor to every 1 800 citizens. In most western nations the ratio is one councillor to between 250 and 450 citizens (Norton 1985, para. 143). The contrast between British practice and that of other democracies is so great that it may be questioned whether Britain has 'local authorities' in the sense in which the phrase is understood elsewhere (Norton 1985, para. 14).

It has been suggested that such relatively low ratios help to keep elected members in close touch with their constituents (Widdicombe 1986e, pp. 140–1). In Sweden, which was one of the countries (like Britain) which instituted radical reductions in the numbers of elected representatives in the 1970s, recent legislation has *increased* the number of councillors in order to reduce the gulf between politicians and voters and to restore personal contacts between them (Gustafson 1983, pp. 30–1).

A relatively low ratio of elected members to citizens is no guarantee that councillors will not feel stressed. The Widdicombe researchers refer to studies in Sweden, Denmark, West Germany and Australia which suggest that the increasing demands of council work have not only required a greater commitment of time but have also placed members under increasing strain. Moreover, they found evidence from New Zealand and Sweden that this growing burden has resulted in an increase in the turnover of councillors (Widdicombe 1986e, p. 142).

There is very little information on the gender composition of local councils. Table 8.2 gives some indication of the extent to which women in some countries have succeeded in gaining a measure of formal political power as elected representatives.

The Nordic countries are often seen as states in which gender equality is most advanced. One recent study concluded, however, that although progress had been made towards greater equality – particularly in the 1960s and 1970s – the proportion of women in the most senior positions on councils was still very small (Haavio-Mannila 1985, p. 105).

Most western democracies have moved away from seeing the role of an elected member of a local authority as requiring no

TABLE 8.2 **Percentage of women on local councils in five Nordic countries and England, Wales and Scotland**

Denmark (1981)	21
Finland (1980)	22
Iceland (1982)	13
Norway (1979)	23
Sweden (1979)	29
England, Wales and Scotland (1985)	19

Sources: Haavio-Mannila *et al.* 1985, p. 91; Widdicombe 1986c, p. 19.

financial help or compensation. In some countries – Denmark, Norway, Sweden and some parts of West Germany – council leaders are paid a full-time salary. In Denmark, for example, a mayor receives a salary in excess of £20 000 a year. In other countries – Australia, USA and France – the emphasis is upon the payment of attendance fees to elected representatives (Widdicombe 1986e, p. 143).

Equally significant is the growing acknowledgement that councillors can play many different roles and can choose to make very different commitments to the work that is involved. This diversity is reflected in the different modes of financial reward or compensation that operate *within* many local government systems and in the fact that councillors (and councils) have some measure of discretion over the amounts paid and what can be legitimately defined as council work.

Sweden is possibly the country that has moved furthest in formally recognising this growing diversity. Councillors are divided into three groups according to the amount of time they invest in their local authority. First, there are full-time councillors or commissioners (of which approximately 7 per cent were women in 1980). They have administrative and managerial duties as well as responsibilities for policy-making and they hold their appointments for the same period of time as the council. Most commissioner positions are taken by the majority party group and carry a salary approximately equal to that of the most senior professional staff employed by the council. The second group are part-time commissioners who devote more than half their working week to the council and are paid accordingly. These full-time and part-time commissioners make up only a small proportion of the 70 000 or so elected members in Sweden, but

> Through their leading position and the publicity they are given by news media, however, they have come to be eminent representatives of their parties and local politics. (Gustafson 1983, p. 94)

The third group – or 'leisure politicians' as they have been described – devote less than half of their time to political activities (Malmsten 1983, p. 8).

Local government legislation in Sweden is aimed at ensuring that diversity of practice is acknowledged. Local authorities have complete freedom of choice concerning the forms in which remuneration is paid and the amount. The law emphasises, however, that the salary must be reasonable in scale. It also permits variations in salaries to allow senior councillors and other members with special duties higher salaries because of the greater amount of work involved (City of Stockholm 1983, p. 11). Councils are also free to grant financial support to political parties. The purpose is to enable parties to create and maintain permanent organisations between elections and to provide political information to the general public. The amount of the party subsidy is directly dependent on the number of council members supporting a party. Recent legislation in Sweden concerning elected members aims at promoting greater diversity of those who are elected and ensuring that all citizens have an equal opportunity to accept local government offices. To this end, entitlement to leave of absence, remuneration, loss of earnings, pensions, child care expenses and financial compensation for those who are disabled or handicapped have received statutory recognition (Gustafson 1983, p. 95).

It is clear from this brief international comparison that British local government is alone amongst local governments in most of the democratic world in experiencing a severe erosion of its powers and influence. Moreover, the number of constituents served by each local representative in Britain is very much higher than in other comparable political systems. Finally, there appears to be a greater readiness to accept that elected members can play a wide variety of different roles, and systems of financial support should match this variety.

Local authorities in the 1990s: the role of councillors

In the Introduction, we highlighted the crisis that confronts local government. Local authorities and their members have, we suggested, been thrust to the centre stage of national and local political debate. For the first time for many years questions about the fundamental purpose of local government have been raised and even its continued existence has been doubted.

Into this debate, however, there has been injected a perspective which was absent in the late 1960s, when the last critical examination of local government occurred. For some years, many people assumed that local authorities should not merely take policy decisions about the services for which Parliament had made them responsible, but that they they should also undertake the delivery and provision of those services. It was widely held that policy-making and provision were inseparable.

The members of the Royal Commissions on Local Government in England and Scotland shared this belief. In the late 1960s they mounted an extensive research programme aimed at answering the question: 'How big are the authorities which *provide* the best services?' The answer the Commissioners received was not, however, the one they wanted. They were told that no clear statistical link could be found between size and performance. In short, bigger was not necessarily better.

Undeterred, and sharing the widespread view that many local authorities were too small, they recommended a structure of local government in which a relatively small number of large authorities were to provide services to substantial populations. Only in this way, many believed, could the 'economies of scale' in the delivery of services be achieved.

The Conservative government of the time did not accept the Royal Commissions' specific recommendations. They did, however, share the widespread assumption that local authorities should be responsible for the provision of services. This could be done with greater efficiency and economy only if most existing authorities were either swept away or amalgamated with their neighbours. The result was the present system of local government about which there is so much intense discussion.

Local authorities: too large, too remote, too bureaucratic

The main antagonists in this debate have a starting point in common. Both Right and Left believe that the local authorities created in the reorganisation of the 1970s are too large, too remote, too 'bureaucratic' and unresponsive. The remedies they advocate, however, could not be more different. The 'New Right' argues for an 'enabling' authority (or alternatively a 'community company') which would provide very little itself but would contract with others (usually private companies) to provide services. The 'New Urban Left' sees the solution in a systematic exposure of the local authority to the opinions and interests of the groups which comprise the local community. By means of such strategies as women's committees, enhanced economic development powers and various forms of decentralised administration and delivery of services, the Left hopes to rejuvenate and protect the idea and practice of the 'providing' authority.

There are many shades of opinion between the polarised conceptions of the enabling authority and the providing authority. Overriding these differences, however, one question has preoccupied both the present government and most of its opponents. This has been the issue of how best to provide services. The government and the 'New Right' see compulsory competitive tendering as the remedy whereby local authorities contract with private companies to provide services. The extension of competitive tendering and the proliferation of companies wholly or partly owned by local authorities means that there will be much greater diversity in the means by which services are delivered to the public. In short, service provision has ceased to be the defining and distinguishing role of local government. The 'efficiency' justification of local government (that only a multi-purpose public body at the local level could efficiently integrate and coordinate service delivery) so beloved by the reformers of the 1960s, has withered in the face of compulsory competitive tendering.

What, if anything, is left if service provision is removed? We argue that community self-government remains the essential justification of local government. The question to be answered should no longer be 'How best can services be provided?' but 'How best to enhance community self government?' (see Stewart in Stewart and Stoker 1989, Ch. 12).

Enhancing community self-government

We have said that the contemporary debate about local government is different from that which occurred in the 1960s insofar as it is no longer unquestioningly assumed that councils should provide and deliver services. We find it remarkable, however, that in the discussions that take place in Parliament, in the press and at the many local government conferences, very little time is devoted to considering the role of the elected representative in the local government of the future. Moreover, most academic observers are preoccupied with the political, financial, managerial and legal implications arising from the very substantial volume of legislation which has affected local authorities in the last decade.

If, as we argue, the only future for local government is community self-government, public debate should focus on how best to develop the essential resource which will make that possible. Discussion should concentrate on the circumstances which enhance the ability and willingness of individuals to participate in the government of the community. As Jones and Stewart have recently argued:

> Representation is a scarce resource in this country and should be cherished and not neglected, in the working of the local authority. (Jones and Stewart 1990)

What do we see as the main implications arising out of our work for this 'scarce resource'? First, we have made it clear that members interpret their council duties in very different ways. We have described three interpretations of these responsibilities – as a hobby, as a vocation and as a job – but we acknowledge the possibility that there may well be greater diversity than we have found. Secondly, we have illustrated with numerous examples, the ways in which many councillors are compelled to play a more attenuated and less committed role than they would otherwise choose because of the conflicting demands of their public and private lives. We suggest, therefore, that future legislation affecting the representative activities of councillors should be framed in the light of two broad related principles:

First, the enhancement of diversity of representation;
Second, the extension of freedom of choice of representative role.

Community self-government and the problem of the recruitment of candidates

The first of these principles draws attention to the availability of people to become candidates at local elections. For the Government, there appears to be no problem. In commending its proposals for a change in the system of remuneration of councillors the White Paper of 1988 the Government said:

There is no evidence of a shortage of candidates for election (except in very rural areas where remuneration is not the principal cause). (Department of the Environment 1988, p. 9)

Political parties face a widespread and recurring problem which their members are more ready to acknowledge in private than in public. Very few people can easily be found to take on a candidature when one falls vacant. We described in Chapter 2 that among active party members there was a significant group of 'resisters' who rejected all forms of persuasion to contest an election. A second group – the 'drifters' – spoke to us about their great reluctance to become candidates and referred to the ways in which they had been 'coerced' or cajoled. This shortage of would-be candidates is less acute where a vacancy occurs in a ward winnable by the governing or majority group. In this situation, party selectors are able to exercise a measure of real choice.

In these 'safe' seats, another aspect of the problem of the recruitment of councillors was evident. Some women we talked to believed that they had detected some prejudice and were strongly in favour of some form of positive discrimination as the only way in which to get an equal proportion of women elected to local councils. (It was in this context that, in one area of our study, such a proposal was put forward, but later rejected.) We would like to endorse the call for positive discrimination in situations where it is warranted, not only in favour of women, but black people and people with disabilities. However, we believe the call for women-only shortlists is misguided, and if put into practice would result in more women being used merely as tokens of equal opportunity.

Other observers have come to similar conclusions regarding the shortage of candidates. Jones and Stewart report that members from all parties find that it is increasingly difficult to find candidates and we wish to support their call for an official inquiry into the availability of candidates (Jones and Stewart 1989).

We have shown that many people, particularly women, are deterred from putting themselves forward because they feel ill-equipped for the job. This is due not so much to lack of skills, but is more a matter of confidence in their own abilities. It is here that encouragement, patience and understanding on the part of party managers can be very important. Some of them may not fully recognise the loss of confidence that often affects people who have given up their paid work to care for their families or who have become unemployed. The prospect of re-entering the world of work can be very intimidating. Women in this position often find classes in 'Returning to Work', assertiveness training and effective communication helpful as a starting point. We suggest, therefore, that local authorities and political parties should offer classes in assertiveness and communication skills as well as training in various aspects of local government to anyone who may be considering becoming politically active.

If we wish to have a larger pool of people from whom to select our local representatives, we must start with a politically aware electorate. The Widdicombe survey of local government electors concluded that nearly half the electorate were 'not very well informed' or 'uninformed' about politics (Widdicombe 1986d, p. 99). These proportions were higher for those with less education, women and young people. In the light of these figures the provision of a broad political education for all schoolchildren should be seen as a priority. This is normal practice in some other countries – for example, in France, and in some of the American states where it is a statutory obligation on the authorities. It is regrettable that this issue did not feature more prominently in discussions concerned with the establishment of a National Curriculum.

Community government and the elected member

In our judgement community government requires both a greater number and a greater diversity of people to put themselves forward for elected office. The measures we have recommended, however, are a necessary but not sufficient part of our answer to the question, What can be done? Training courses of various kinds and improved education are very valuable in removing obstacles preventing people from becoming politically active. Yet such changes are unlikely to be effective if local authorities are neither free nor willing to adapt to the greater diversity of representative roles that we have advocated.

Every local authority could immediately introduce certain practical measures which would require neither government approval nor large resources. Together with other observers, we feel that members need a much wider range of support services. Moreover, these must be available at convenient times. We have already noted (in Chapter 3) that in 1982 there was a widespread lack of secretarial assistance and since that time there has been no significant improvement. Without administrative support many members are effectively denied the chance to adopt one or other of the more demanding councillor roles. In this regard, we do not see the provisions in the 1989 Local Government and Housing Act allowing the employment of a maximum of three 'political assistants' for party groups as likely to bring any significant improvement.

Information technology might be used to provide both better administrative support and up-to-date and accessible information for members. In recent years, there has been a massive influx of information technology into local government – a sevenfold increase in expenditure since 1980. It appears that the technology has been seen primarily as an aid for officers rather than councillors. Fewer than 5 per cent of councillors have access to computer-based information at home. Moreover, this does not seem to be due to members' reluctance to change. In a recent survey, 1 in 5 councillors said that they would welcome home-access to their council's databases. Moreover, computer literacy does not appear to be too great an obstacle. Sixty per cent of councillors in employment use computer information in their paid work. We think it is significant that where home-access has been introduced it has proved extremely popular with councillors but correspondingly unpopular with officers. This is largely because of the number of requests for data and questions on specific issues that have flowed from the increased access! (International Computers Limited 1988, pp. 20–2). We see no reason why the local authority associations could not initiate an inquiry into the greater use by councillors of this technology in conjunction with those suppliers of hardware and software which have found local government to be so profitable a market.

'A remarkably low price for a system of democratic representation'

The Widdicombe Report remarked that the evidence on the remuneration arrangements for members had been more emphatic than on any other issue. Almost all who commented said that the arrangements were unsatisfactory both in terms of the basis of the payment and the level of payment (Widdicombe 1986a, p. 129).

Much of the evidence to the Widdicombe inquiry on this matter revealed the great difficulty that many people have in finding a real analogy for the role of the councillor. Should councillors be seen as representatives of the local community carrying out a public duty in very much the same way as someone, say, on jury service? As such they should be compensated for any loss incurred as a result of carrying out those duties, but should not be remunerated in the sense of having a monetary value placed on their work.

Alternatively, it is widely argued that, in the light of the considerable size and complexity (in terms of organisation, budget and geographical area) of many local authorities, senior councillors such as leaders and the holders of committee chairs are carrying out major statutory responsibilities which in other comparable contexts would entail very substantial remuneration.

Accordingly, Widdicombe proposed a much simplified system of remuneration based on two elements:

– a basic flat-rate allowance (payable to all members but varying according to the population of the authority's area);
– a special responsibility allowance (to be mandatory) available for 'key' councillors.

The basic flat rate allowance was to replace the financial loss allowance and the attendance allowance. (In Chapter 6, we referred to the criticisms of attendance allowances which were made by both the Robinson and Widdicombe Committees and by many of the councillors we interviewed.)

The Widdicombe Committee estimated that the total annual cost of the system it proposed would be about £56 million – an increase of £36.5 million on the level of spending in 1985–86. The Committee commented:

> No recommendation involving an increase in public expenditure is welcome. Even, however, after the increase the total cost of allowances would represent under 0.2% of local authority rate and grant borne expenditure. We believe this is a remarkably low price for a system of democratic representation. (Widdicombe 1986a, p. 134)

The proposed new system of councillors' allowances

In 1990 a new system of allowances was proposed, but its implementation has been delayed. Each council would determine the maximum it could spend on allowances by multiplying the appropriate figure in Table 8.3 by the number of councillors.

TABLE 8.3 Members' allowances (maxima per authority)

Metropolitan districts	£2550
London Boroughs and county councils	£2550
Shire district councils with a population of less than 170 000	£1250
Shire district councils with a population of more than 170 000	£1800
Metropolitan joint authorities	£800

Source: Department of the Environment, The Local Authorities (Members' Allowances) Regulations 1990.

Two kinds of payment would be required to be made from the total amount available for each council. Firstly, the Special Responsibility Allowance (which was a optional feature of the old system) would remain. However, instead of prescribing the maximum absolute amount that could be paid (both per person and per authority), the government stipulates that the minimum and maximum amounts available for the SRA are defined as 5 per cent and 25 per cent respectively of the total estimated allowances. SRAs would be payable to a maximum of five members or one-third of the council, whichever is greater, and no member could receive more than £7500 from this source. Where an authority is divided into majority and minority groups, at least one SRA would be paid to a member who is not in the majority group. The amount of this allowance – essentially for the leader of the largest minority group on a council – could not be less than the lowest amount paid to other members who receive an SRA. Secondly, as an innovation, there would be a Basic Allowance payable equally to all members the aggregate of which could not be less than 25 per cent of the total available for allowances.

A third allowance – an Attendance Allowance – could be paid at the discretion of a council for members carrying out 'approved duties', i.e. attending council and committee meetings. Where an authority is divided into two or more party groups, this allowance could be paid only if members from at least two such groups had been invited. Where an Attendance Allowance is paid it could not exceed £21 per day (in 1990–1). Finally, the financial loss allowance (a feature of the old system) was to be discontinued. A council could amend its scheme of allowances in the course of the financial year to which it relates.

The proposed system: implications for diversity and choice

What are the implications of this proposal? Clearly the discretionary features of the system are such that it is difficult to predict how local councils will divide the total sums they are entitled to spend within the various prescribed statutory limits.

At this stage, however, a number of comments can be made. The system would rest on a new series of controls over an area of local authority expenditure which has in the past been largely discretionary and which itself is a very small proportion of total local authority expenditure. While there has been criticism of the attendance allowance, there has been no serious criticism that the money spent by local authorities has been too high.

The government's view has been that there is no reason to increase expenditure. For the first year of operation, therefore, the government has anticipated allocating £45.2 million to the scheme. This can be compared with the cost of the Widdicombe proposals which (when adjusted for inflation) would be in excess of £75 millions. This is a measure of the low value placed by the government on the activities of councillors and the limited extent to which it wishes to encourage active citizenship. We would endorse the combined view of the local authority associations:

> The Associations' concern is to maintain a healthy, efficient and effective local democracy. The fear is that this will become increasingly difficult if the commitment and hard work undertaken in the cause of public service, is not recognised or adequately valued. Above all, the financial consequences of service on a Council should not become a powerful disincentive to participation in local government; especially given the desirability of encouraging a variety of councillors from all walks of life, representative of their communities in the round. The aggregate quantum proposed is actually a very small element of expenditure when seen in the context of the services for which local government is responsible. (Local Authority Associations 1989)

As we have said, the effect of fixing a global amount would be, for the first time, to place a cash-limit on local authorities in terms of how much they could spend on allowances. Councils which have in the past spent above these limits were to be given three years to come into line and to adopt, in effect, the government's definition and valuation of members' activities.

The cash-limit is likely to have a further consequence for members' activities. Many local authorities, when faced with difficult and unforeseen problems or highly contentious or complex issues have found a need to arrange additional meetings of committees and sub-committees. They are also, in many instances, under a statutory obligation to hold consultative meetings with the public, with the users of a service (such as parents in the case of a school closure) and with business groups. In these circumstances, where an authority has not continued with an attendance allowance or where only a small residual sum has been allocated for that purpose, the ability of the council to meet the *extra* costs arising would either be very limited or would require a fundamental amendment of its scheme. This lack of flexibility in the face of the unforeseen or the exceptional is likely to curtail members' ability to respond.

In a similar fashion, the government's definition of 'approved duties' for the purpose of the attendance allowance is likely to cause practical difficulties at the ward level. As we have seen, an activity could be defined as an 'approved duty' only if, *inter alia*, members from two or more party groups have been invited. It is easy to see the absurdity of this requirement. A site meeting in a ward represented by members from the same political party could become an approved duty only when a member from another party (and another ward) is invited!

No less absurd is the implication of this requirement for local authorities where the opposition group may comprise a very small number of members. (One of the county councils in our survey was in this situation.) The effect would be to inundate those few members with 'invitations' in order to adhere to the letter of the regulations. Minority group members, already hard-pressed to attend the most important committees, are unlikely to see much sense in this provision.

The proposed removal of the financial loss allowance from elected members (but not from appointed members such as magistrates on police committees and co-opted members on education committees) seems to us a unnecessary restriction. It is clear that the government seized the opportunity presented by the research undertaken for the Widdicombe inquiry and the conclusions reached by that Committee in this regard. We endorse the Committee's comment that

> It is invidious that a wage-earner and someone looking after a home should put in similar hours but that only the former should be remunerated. (Widdicombe 1986a, p. 130)

We feel, however, that the government (and Widdicombe) have moved in the wrong direction. As we said in Chapter 6, the financial loss allowance was taken up by only a few members, but it could make all the difference in enabling some members to avoid serious financial detriment as a direct consequence of being a councillor. Its existence encouraged and modestly widened the representative nature of local government. We feel it should be retained and that councils should have been given the choice of extending it to provide financial recompense for those councillors with responsibility for young children and other dependent family members.

We saw in Chapter 6 that some councillors we spoke to, for example those who were unemployed, faced particular difficulties with regard to their entitlement to certain social security payments. Widdicombe, also, found that many councillors had been adversely affected in this way but concluded that this issue was beyond their remit (Widdicombe 1986a, p. 132). The government declared that:

> Membership of a local authority is not a salaried appointment or post. (Department of the Environment 1988)

It has not, however, sought to reverse by legislation the judgement of the Appeal Court in 1985 that acting as a local authority councillor in respect of which an attendance allowance is paid constitutes work as defined under the Social Security Act 1975. Moreover, at the time of writing, the promised working party between the Department of the Environment, the Department of Social Security and the Inland Revenue has yet to meet.

Our judgement of the proposed system of allowances is clear. We do not see these provisions as likely to bring about the fundamental change in the position of elected members which we are advocating. Indeed, other recent legislation places new legal constraints on the actions of councillors. Local authorities are required to designate certain of their officers to play a monitoring and scrutinising role and to act independently of elected members in certain circumstances. The judgement of members is not, in the government's view, to be trusted.

Towards radical change?

Earlier in this chapter, we mentioned a variety of measures – such as improved political education in the schools – which we believe would contribute, in the long term, to the rejuvenation of local democracy. We do not wish to imply, however, that, in the further proposals which follow, the solution lies solely in the hands of future legislators. Many decades of growing centralisation and the hiving-off of certain functions to non-elected agencies have lowered the electorate's expectations of local democracy. Both tendencies have bred an inertia and indifference in many voters which is not something that can be remedied by Act of Parliament.

Not only is legislation ineffective in the face of a culture of indifference. A surfeit of legislation is part of the problem. For more than a decade, Parliament has, on average, passed ten major Acts per year affecting, and usually constraining, local government. We hope that a new government and a new Parliament will achieve a better balance between its legal capacity to pass laws and its deeply-flawed knowledge of the world beyond London. If some measure of self-restraint does not emerge, the demand for a statement of constitutional principle – a Charter of Local Authority Rights, perhaps – will grow.

A self-denying ordinance on the part of 'metropolitan policy-makers' would be a necessary first step towards making the local representative role more meaningful – perhaps a return to the separate worlds of 'High' and 'Low' politics which we mentioned in Chapter 1. Put simply, it would create some space within which local democracy could grow.

Such growth can occur if local authorities are able to pay some, at least, of their members a salary the level of which could be determined in a fashion similar to that of MPs, i.e. it would be linked to a particular point on the salary scale of local government officers and broadly in line with the payments made to the Chairs of health authorities (£18 000 per annum). These members would be the full-time professional local politicians who would have an involvement in the detailed implementation of policies similar to that of ministers in London. We see no reason why such public service should not count towards a pension after the completion, say, of two terms of office.

For other councillors, those who wish to make a major but not a full-time contribution and those 'leisure politicians' whose commitment is much more limited, we see most merit in a reformed system of attendance allowances. These allowances should be clearly available for a wide range of approved duties and should include such essential activities as ward surgeries, meetings with community groups and public consultation meetings organised by the council. We believe it is essential that this allowance is linked to the retail price index to ensure that its real value is not again allowed to decline. As we have said above, we see costs incurred in looking after dependants as best recompensed through a modified financial loss allowance.

The remuneration of councillors is, however, only one side of the financial significance of local representation. As we said in Chapter 6, members who are in employment are sometimes subject to penalties such as lack of promotion prospects and serious loss of earnings. From the perspective of the employer, we find it understandable that the regular and frequent absence of an employee on council business is likely to have an adverse effect on such matters as production, sales, despatch of customer's orders, planning and management, and may also increase the pressures on other workers. We think that where significant financial loss can be demonstrated by an employer (and we anticipate that this will be most readily shown in the case of small businesses where the absence of an employee will be most felt) there should be means of recompense available.

What would happen to the job of an employee who became a full-time professional politician? In this situation, we think that if that person lost all claim on the job by virtue of being elected, it would inevitably deter some people from becoming candidates in the first place. We therefore suggest that the job should remain available for the employee to return to after one period of office, i.e. four years. This would have the incidental but important benefit of providing more employment opportunities of sufficient duration to make it worthwhile for employers to train the temporary worker.

While we suggest that these measures will enhance diversity and choice they are necessarily piecemeal in character. What is needed is an institution with a genuine independence similar to that of the Audit Commission. A Standing Commission for Local Representation could absorb the functions and duties of the Local Government Boundary Commission and the Commission for Local Administration but, most importantly, act as an authoritative adviser to the government and local authorities on all matters relating to local representation. For example, it would be free to comment on school curricula, on electoral arrangements, on the likely impact on local representation of bills passing through Parliament and legislation emerging from the European Parliament and the European Commission. It could review and advise on the law as it relates to local councillors, candidates and political parties. It could initiate inquiries and sponsor research as its commissioners thought appropriate.

None of these measures are, however, likely to have much relevance if local government is compelled to follow the very restricted model of the 'enabling authority' or the 'community company' meeting very infrequently with the limited function of awarding contracts for services. This notion rests on a simplistic vision of the future wherein local authorities' responsibilities are almost unthinkingly discharged by the operation of markets and price mechanisms – that is, what is cheapest is necessarily the best. The occasional opportunity to award a contract will do nothing to solve the problems of candidate recruitment faced by the political parties.

Our own view does not rest, we hope, on such naïve simplicities. As we move into the twenty-first century, local authorities face problems of unprecedented complexity. They confront, for example, such diverse issues as community care, transportation and the environment. If they are to be successful, they will need to attract able people from all parts of the communities they serve. To do so, these people should be allowed discretion and meaningful choice. Without the changes we have suggested, the decline in local democracy will become irreversible.

Appendix: Conducting and Analysing the Interviews

The data for this book came from two separate studies undertaken between 1984 and 1988. Both studies were based upon semi-structured interviews (see below) with local politicians and their spouses or other partners. For the first study we interviewed 65 county councillors and their partners from three different authorities in the south-west; the second study, also based in the south-west, comprised 45 women (and their partners) who were active in their local communities but were not councillors. In the first study we also used self-completion diaries.

Given the innovative character of our work, we aimed to cast our net as widely possible to capture the greatest possible diversity of experience. In constructing the first sample, however, we encountered an interesting problem – that local authorities keep very little information about their elected representatives. The councils we approached readily gave us information about councillors' main committee memberships, party and gender, but they did not have any information, for example, about members' marital or occupational statuses. Consequently, we chose equal numbers of men and women councillors, equal numbers of leading councillors (whom we called Chairs) and backbenchers, and representatives from the political groups proportional to their numbers on the respective councils.

We decided, in the light of the nature and extent of the material we wished to cover, that we would try to interview councillors on two occasions. This also enabled us to discuss with each member some of the entries in the diary. Of the 65 councillors initially approached, 62 agreed to be interviewed and 60 were interviewed twice. We also interviewed separately the partners of 54 of the councillors, most of the remainder being unmarried and having no other identifiable partner. We conducted these interviews in 1985 –

211

approximately half before and half following the county council elections of that year.

Our findings from this first study influenced the composition of the sample in the second study. When looking at the interrelationships between the public and private sides of councillors' lives the gender of the councillor was understandably of crucial importance. It was clear that women had to be particularly careful to keep a balance between the demands of their council role and the responsibilities they might have outside that – for example, to their jobs and their homes. At the same time we were aware that the well-established statistical under-representation of women on local councils demanded some explanation. Was it possible that many women activists were aware of the potential difficulties of council membership, and, in consequence, were very reluctant even to consider standing as candidates in local elections?

The size of our second sample was unfortunately constrained by financial restrictions. We decided, therefore, to focus on women and to explore their attitudes regarding standing for the council. We wanted to talk to women who were active in political parties and community groups, only a small minority of whom were prepared to become candidates at local elections. Accordingly, we approached 26 women who had been selected as candidates for the district council elections of May 1987, and 19 women (the 'non-candidates') who, though active in their community or party, were not standing in the elections and had not stood previously. All the women lived within one county in the south-west of England and their political sympathies were roughly equally divided between the major parties. We interviewed 45 of the 48 women we approached and 32 of the 38 partners.

In studies of this kind it is particularly important to establish a good relationship with informants. Almost without exception we were warmly welcomed. Many interviews lasted longer than we had originally anticipated and a number of people remarked on how they had found the interview a rewarding experience. In some cases, the politicians and their partners felt free to impart sensitive information or express a long-held sense of grievance which they had not felt able to tell anyone else. To that extent the interviews may have been therapeutic.

Most of the interviews followed a loosely-structured schedule, which covered such subjects as: family composition; employment;

history of political and community involvement; leisure activities and social relationships; household division of labour; and, where appropriate, the steps leading up to a candidacy; current council workload; and future plans. We encouraged people to speak freely on the subjects which particularly concerned *them* and probed as appropriate to fill out a picture of their varied public and private lives.

Most of the people we spoke to were understandably concerned about the confidential nature of some of the matters covered in the interviews. In order to preserve this confidentiality we have disguised the identity of our informants and use pseudonyms for those people we quote.

We tape-recorded the interviews and transcribed them into a Prime mainframe computer. We then extracted the relevant factual data, e.g. the age of the informant, and entered this into the computer for later cross-referencing against the more qualitative material. We coded all interviews, working in groups of two or three, and built up a consensus of interpretation. These codes were then inserted into the appropriate computer transcripts. This allowed us to analyse the material in terms of particular themes, e.g. social life, workload, partner support. We also wrote individual 'profiles' of our subjects to ensure that we did not lose sight of the unique character of each respondent. Further details of our methodology, including copies of the interview schedules we used, are included in our two reports:

'Married to the Council?' The Private Costs of Public Service. A Report to the Leverhulme Trust. (1987; ISBN 0–904951–63–4).

Resistance and Drift: Women Entering Local Politics. (1988; ISBN 0–871056–05–5).

Bibliography

Alexander, A. (1982), *Local Government in Britain since Reorganisation* (Allen and Unwin).

Askham, J. (1984), *Identity and Stability in Marriage* (Cambridge University Press).

Association of Councillors (1987), *Support Services for Councillors* (Association of Councillors).

Association of District Councils (1989), *Meeting Housing Needs* (Association of District Councils).

Audit Commission (1984), *The Impact on Local Authorities' Economy, Efficiency and Effectiveness of the Block Grant Distribution System* (HMSO).

Audit Commission (1986), *Attitudes to Local Authorities and Their Services* (HMSO).

Audit Commission (1989), *Housing the Homeless: The Local Authority Role* (HMSO).

Bains Report (1972), *The New Local Authorities: Management and Structure* (HMSO).

Barber, J. (1965), *The Lawmakers* (Yale University Press).

Barron, J. (1989), *Gender, Class and Politics: Women in the Labour and Conservative Parties* (Unpublished PhD thesis, University College of Wales, Cardiff).

Barron, J., Crawley, G. and Wood, T. (1987), *Married to the Council? The Private Costs of Public Service. A Report to the Leverhulme Trust.* (Bristol Polytechnic).

Barron, J., Crawley, G. and Wood, T. (1988), *Resistance and Drift: Women Entering Politics* (Bristol Polytechnic).

Barron, J., Crawley, G. and Wood, T. (1989), 'Drift and Resistance: Refining Models of Political Recruitment', *Policy and Politics*, Vol. 17, no. 3 (pp. 207–19).

Berger, P. and Kellner (1964), 'Marriage and the Construction of Reality'. Reprinted in Anderson, M. (ed.) (1980), *Sociology of the Family* 2nd ed. (Penguin).

Bernard, J. (1972), *The Future of Marriage* (Souvenir Press).

Black, G. (1972), 'A Theory of Political Ambition', *American Political Science Review* Vol. 66, no. 1.

Blair, D. and Henry, A. (1981), 'The Family Factor in State and Legislative Turnover', *Legislative Studies Quarterly* 1 (pp. 55–68).

Blood, R. O. and Wolfe, D. (1965), *Husbands and Wives: The Dynamics of Modern Living* (Free Press).

Bochel, J. (1966), 'The Recruitment of Local Councillors: A Case Study', *Political Studies*, Vol. 14, no. 3 (pp. 360–4).

Boddy, M. and Fudge, C. (eds.) (1984), *Local Socialism* (Macmillan).

Bott, E. (1971), *Family and Social Network* 2nd ed. (Free Press).

Boulton, M. G. (1983), *On Being a Mother: A Study of Women with Pre-School Children* (Tavistock).

Brand, J. (1973), 'Party Organisation and the Recruitment of Councillors', *British Journal of Political Science*, Vol. 3, no. 4 (pp. 473–86).

Breton, A. and Wintrobe, R., (1982), *The Logic of Bureaucratic Conduct: Economic Analysis of Competition, Exchange and Efficiency in Private and Public Organisations* (Cambridge University Press).

Bristow, S. (1980), 'Women Councillors: An Explanation of the Under-Representation of Women in Local Government', *Local Government Studies*, May/June 1980.

Bristow, S. *et al.* (1983), *The Redundant Counties* (Hesketh).

Bryant, B., Harkis, M., and Newton, D. (1980), *Children and their Minders* (Grant McIntyre).

Budge, I., Brand, J., Margolis, M. and Smith, A. (1972), *Political Stratification and Democracy* (Macmillan).

Budge, I. and Fairlie, D. (1975), 'Political Recruitment and Drop-Out: Predictive Success of Background Characteristics over Five British Localities', *British Journal of Political Science*, Vol. 5, no. 1 (pp. 33–58).

Bulpitt, J. (1983), *Territory and Power* (Manchester University Press).

Callan, H. and Ardener, S. (1984), *The Incorporated Wife* (Croom Helm).

Cavendish, R. (1982), *Women on the Line* (Routledge and Kegan Paul).

Central Policy Review Staff (1977), *Relations between Central Government and Local Authorities* (HMSO).

Central Statistical Office (1988), *Social Trends No. 18* (HMSO).

Chandler, J. A. (1988), Public Policy-Making for Local Government (Croom Helm).

Cicourel, A. (1964), *Method and Measurement in Sociology* (Collier-Macmillan).

CIPFA (1989), *Local Government Trends* (Chartered Institute of Public Finance and Accountancy).

City of Stockholm (1983), *Local Self-Government in Stockholm*.

Clarke and Stewart, A. (1982), *Day Care* (Fontana).

Clements, R. (1969), *Local Notables and the City Council* (Macmillan).

Collins, C. A. (1978a), 'Social Background and Motivation of Councillors', *Policy and Politics* 6, pp. 425–7.

Collins, C. A. (1978b), 'The Officer and Councillor in Local Government', *Public Administration Bulletin*, No. 28.

Commission for Local Administration (1987), *Annual Report* (CLA).

Consumers' Association (1989), *Which?*, March 1989.

Council of Europe (1981), *Functional Decentralisation at Local and Regional Level* (Council of Europe).

Crawford, M. (1977), 'What is a Friend?', *New Society* 20 October 1977 (pp. 116–17).

Dearlove, J. (1973), *The Politics of Policy in Local Government* (Cambridge University Press).

Dearlove, J. (1979), *Reorganisation of British Local Government* (Cambridge University Press).

Deaux, K. (1976), *Behaviour of Women and Men* (Brooks/Cole).

Deem, R. (1986), *All Work and No Play?* (Open University Press).

Deem, R. and Salaman, G. (1985), *Work, Culture and Society* (Open University Press).

Department of Environment (1971a), Green Paper: *The Future Shape of Local Government Finance* (HMSO).

Department of Environment (1971b), White Paper: *Local Government in England. Government Proposals for Reorganisation* (HMSO).

Department of Environment (1986), *Paying for Local Government* (HMSO).

Department of Environment (1988), White Paper: *The Conduct of Local Authority Business* (HMSO).

Department of Environment (1990), *The Local Authorities (Members' Allowances) Regulations* (HMSO).

Dex, S. (1988), *Women's Attitudes Towards Work* (Macmillan).

Dunleavy, P. and Rhodes, R. A. W. (1988), 'Government Beyond Whitehall', in Drucker, H. (1988), *Developments in British Politics* (Macmillan).

Duverger, Maurice (1955), *The Political Role of Women* (UNESCO).

Eddison, T., Fudge, C., Murie, A. and Ring, E. (1978), *Strengthening the Role of the Elected Member* (Bristol: School of Advanced Urban Studies).

Edgell, S. (1980), *Middle Class Couples: A Study in Segregation, Domination and Inequality in Marriage* (Allen and Unwin).

Elcock, H. (1982), *Local Government: Politicians, Professionals and Public in Local Authorities* (Methuen).

Evans, J. (1984), 'The Good Society? Implications of a Greater Participation by Women in Public Life', *Political Studies*, Vol. 34 (pp. 618–26).

Finch. J. (1983), *Married to the Job: Wives' Incorporation in Men's Work* (Allen and Unwin).

Fonda, N. and Moss, P. (1976) (ed.), *Mothers in Employment* (Brunel University).

Fowlkes, M. (1980), *Behind Every Successful Woman: Wives of Medicine and Academe* (Columbia University Press).

Fudge, C., Murie, and Ring, E. (1979), *First Steps to a Career* (Bristol: School of Advanced Urban Studies).

Gail, S. (1985), 'Housewife', in Littler, G. (ed.), *The Experience of Work* (Gower/Heinemann).

Gavron, H. (1966), *The Captive Wife* (Penguin).

Ginsberg, S. (1976), 'Women, Work, and Conflict', in Fonda and Moss (ed.), op. cit.

Glaser, B. and Strauss, A. (1967), *The Discovery of Grounded Theory* (Aldine).

Gordon, I. (1979), 'The Recruitment of Local Politicians: An Integrated Approach with some Preliminary Findings from a Study of Labour Councillors', *Policy and Politics*, Vol. 7, no. 1 (pp. 1–37).

Gregory, S. (1982), 'Women Among Others: Another View', *Journal of Leisure Studies*, Vol. 1, no. 1.

Griffin, C., Hobson, D., McIntosh, S. and McCabe, T. (1982), 'Women and Leisure', in Hargreaves, J. (ed.), *Sport, Culture and Ideology* (Routledge and Kegan Paul).

Gustafson, A. (1983), *Local Government in Sweden* (Stockholm: Swedish Institute).

Gyford, J. (1984), *Local Politics in Britain* (Croom Helm).

Gyford, J., Leach, S. and Game, C. (1989), *The Changing Politics of Local Government* (Unwin Hyman).

Haavio-Mannilla, E. *et al.* (1985), *Unfinished Democracy: Women in Nordic Politics* (Pergamon).

Heclo, H. (1969), 'The Councillor's Job', *Public Administration* (pp. 185–202).

Henwood, M., Rimmer, L., and Wicks, M. (1987), *Inside the Family* (Family Policy Studies Institute).

Hills, J. (1978a), 'Discrimination against Women in the Labour Party', Paper given at Political Science Association Conference, Spring 1978.

Hills, J. (1978b), 'Women in the Labour and Conservative Parties', Paper given at Political Science Association Conference, Spring 1978.

Hills, J. (1980), 'Lifestyle Constraints on Formal Political Participation: Why So Few Women Local Government Councillors in Britain?', Paper presented to the Annual Meeting of the American Political Science Association, 1980 (Washington, DC).

Hills, J. (1981), 'Candidates: The Impact of Gender', *Parliamentary Affairs*, Vol. 34, no. 2 (pp. 221–8).

Horner, M. (1972), 'Towards an Understanding of Achievement Related Conflicts in Women', *Journal of Social Issues* 28, 2 (pp. 151–75).

House of Commons (1988), Employment Committee, Third Report, *The Employment Effects of Urban Development Corporations* (HMSO).

House of Commons (1990), *Hansard* 4 September 1990, Written Answers, Cols 476–678.

International Computers Ltd (1988), *Local Government in Britain: An ICL Report of the Impact of Information Technology*.

Jennings, M. K. (1979), 'Another Look at the Life Cycle and Political Participation', *American Journal of Political Science*, Vol. 23, no. 4.

Jennings, M. K. and Niemi, R. G. (1981), *Generations and Politics: A Panel Study of Young Adults and their Parents* (Princeton University Press).

Jennings, R. E. (1982), 'Changing Representational Role of Local Councillors in England', *Local Government Studies*, Vol. 8, no. 5 (pp. 67–86).

Jephcott, P. *et al.* (1962), *Married Women Working* (Allen and Unwin).

Johnson, F. L. and Aries, E. J. (1983), 'The Talk of Women Friends', *Women's Studies International Forum*, Vol. 6, no. 4 (pp. 353–61).

Jones, G. W. (1969), *Borough Politics* (Macmillan).

Jones, G. W. (1973), 'The Functions and Organisation of Councillors', *Public Administration*, Vol. 51, no. 2 (pp. 135–46).

Jones, G. and Stewart, J. (1983), *The Case for Local Government* (Allen and Unwin).

Jones, G. and Stewart, J. (1989), 'Seven Ways Forward for a Better Future', *Local Government Chronicle*, 10 November 1989.

Jones, G. and Stewart, J. (1990), 'Representative Quality under Threat', *Local Government Chronicle*, 12 January 1990.

Jowell, R. and Witherspoon, S. (1985), *British Social Attitudes: The 1985 Report* (Gower).

Klein, V. (1965), *Britain's Married Women Workers* (Routledge and Kegan Paul).

Kurth, S. (1970), 'Friendships and Friendly Relations', in .McCall, G. (ed.), *Social Relationships* (Aldine).

Lane, R. (1959), *Political Life* (Free Press of Glencoe).

Leach, S. (1989), 'Strengthening Local Democracy? The Government's Response to Widdicombe', in Stewart, J. and Stoker, G. (ed), *The Future of Local Government* (Macmillan).

Lee, J. M. (1963), *Social Leaders and Public Persons* (Oxford University Press).

Lewis, N., Seneviratne, M., and Cracknell, S. (1987), *Complaints Procedures in Local Government*, Vols I and II (Centre for Criminological and Socio-legal Studies, University of Sheffield).

Littler, G. (1985) (ed.), *The Experience of Work* (Gower/Heinemann).

Local Authority Associations (1989), *Briefing for House of Lords Report Stage* (Local Authority Associations, 18 January 1989).

Loughlin, M. (1985), 'The Restructuring of Central-Local Government Legal Relations', *Local Government Studies*, November/December.

Lynn, N. and Flora, C. (1973), 'Motherhood and Political Participation: The Changing Sense of Self', *Journal of Political and Military Sociology*, Vol. 1 (pp. 91–103).

McGrew, A. and Bristow, S. (1983), 'Candidate to Councillor', in Bristow *et al.*, op. cit.

McLaren, P. (1987), *Political Recruitment: A Literature Review Spanning Twenty-Five Years of Studies and Investigations; The First Step in Constructing a Workable Model* (Occasional Papers in Economics and Politics, no. 88/1. Trent Polytechnic).

MacLennan Report (1989), *The Nature and Effectiveness of Housing Management in England* (HMSO).

Malmston, B. (1983), 'Sweden's Salaried Local Politicians', in *Local Government Studies*, May/June 1983.

Mansfield, P. and Collard, J. (1988), *The Beginning of the Rest of Your Life? A Portrait of Newly-Wed Marriage* (Macmillan).

MORI (Market and Opinion Research International) (1986), *Attitudes to Local Authorities and Their Services* (MORI).

Martlew, C., Forrester, C. and Buchanan, G. (1985), 'Activism and Office: Women and Local Government in Scotland', *Local Government Studies*, March/April 1985.

Martlew, C. (1988), *Local Democracy in Practice* (Avebury).

Mather, G. (1989), 'Thatcherism and Local Government: An Evaluation', in Stewart, J. and Stoker, G. (ed.), *The Future of Local Government* (Macmillan).

Matza, D. (1964), *Delinquency and Drift* (Wiley).

Maud (1967a), *Committee on the Management of Local Government*, Vol. 1 Report (HMSO).

Maud (1967b), *Committee on the Management of Local Government*, Vol. 2 The Local Government Councillor (HMSO).

Maud (1967c), *Committee on the Management of Local Government*, Vol. 3 The Local Government Elector (HMSO).

Means, I. (1971), *Norwegian Recruitment Patterns and the Recruitment of Women* PhD thesis, University of Washington.

Milbrath, L. (1965), *Political Participation: How and Why do People get involved in Politics?* (Rand McNally).

Miller, W. (1988), *Irrelevant Elections?* (Oxford University Press).

Mortimer, J., Hall, R. and Hill, R. (1978), 'Husbands' occupational attributes and constraints on wives' employment', *Sociology of Work and Occupations*, Vol. 5, no. 3 (pp. 285–313).

Myrdal, A. and Klein, V. (1956), *Women's two roles* 2nd ed. (Routledge and Kegan Paul).

National Audit Office (1985), Report by the Comptroller and Auditor General. *Operation of the Rate Support Grant System* (NAO).

Newson, J. and Newson, E. (1963), *Infant Care in an Urban Community* (Penguin).

Newson, J. and Newson, E. (1970), *Four Years Old in an Urban Community* (Penguin).

Newson, J. and Newson, E. (1976), *Seven Years Old in the Home Environment* (Allen and Unwin).

Newton, K. (1974), 'Role Orientations and their Sources among Elected Representatives in English Local Politics', *Journal of Politics*, Vol. 36 (pp. 615–36).

Newton, K. (1976), *Second City Politics* (Oxford University Press).

Niskanen, W. (1973), *Bureaucracy: Servant or Master?* (Institute of Economic Affairs).

Norton, A. (1985), *Local Government in Other Western Democracies*, (Institute of Local Government Studies, University of Birmingham).

Oakley, A. (1974), *Sociology of Housework* (Martin Robertson).

Oakley, A. (1976), *Housewife* (Penguin).

Pahl, R. (1984), *Divisions of Labour* (Blackwell).

Pahl, R. and Pahl, J. (1971), *Managers and their Wives* (Allen Lane).

Papanek, H. (1973), 'Men, Women and Work: Reflections on the Two-Person Career', *American Journal of Sociology*, Vol. 78, no. 4 (pp. 852–72).

Parker, S. (1972), *The Future of Work and Leisure* (Paladin).

Parker, S. (1983), *Leisure and Work* (Allen and Unwin).
Philpott, T. (1974), 'A New Councillor's Cry from the Heart About his Job', *Municipal Review*, Vol. 45, July 1974, p. 122.
Pirie, M. (1982), *The Logic of Economics* (Adam Smith Institute).
Pollert, A. (1981), *Girls, Wives, Factory Lives* (Macmillan).
Radice, L., Vallance, E. and Willis, V. (1987), *Member of Parliament: The Job of a Backbencher* (Macmillan).
Rallings, C. and Thrasher, M. (1988), *1988 Local Elections Handbook*, Vols I and II (Plymouth Polytechnic).
Randall, V. (1987), *Women in Politics: An International Perspective*, 2nd ed. (Macmillan).
Rapoport, R. and Rapoport, R. (1971), *Dual Career Families* (Penguin).
Rees, A. and Smith, J. (1964), *Town Councillors: A Study of Barking* (London: Acton Society Trust).
Rhodes, R. A. W. (1985), 'Intergovernmental Relations in the Post-War Period', *Local Government Studies*, November/December.
Ridley, N. (1988), *The Local Right* (Centre for Policy Studies).
Robinson Committee (1977), *Remuneration of Councillors*, Vol. 1 Report, Vol. 2 The Surveys of Councillors and Local Authorities (HMSO).
Rose, R. (1962), 'The Political Ideals of English Party Activists', *American Political Science Review*, Vol. 56, no. 2 (pp. 413–15).
Royal Commission on Local Government in England (1969), *Report*, Vol. 1 (HMSO).
Salmon, Lord (1976) (Chair) *Report of the Royal Commission on Standards of Conduct in Public Life* (HMSO).
Sapiro, V. (1982), 'Private Costs of Public Commitments or Public Costs of Private Commitments? Family Roles versus Political Ambition', *American Journal of Political Science*, Vol. 26, no. 2 (pp. 265–79).
Schwartz, D. C. (1969), 'Towards a Theory of Political Recruitment', *Western Political Quarterly*, Vol. 22, Part 3 (pp. 552–71).
Searing, D. (1985), 'The Role of the Good Constituency Member: The Practice of Representation in Britain', *Journal of Politics*, Vol. 47 (pp. 348–81).
Sharpe, L. (1962), 'Elected Representatives in Local Government', *British Journal of Sociology*, Vol. 13 (pp. 195–209).
Siltanen, J. and Stanworth, M. (1984) (eds), *Women in the Public Sphere* (Hutchinson).
Sinkkonen, S. *et al.* (1985), 'Women in Local Politics', in Haavio-Manila, E. *et al.* (eds), *Unfinished Democracy in Nordic Politics* (Pergamon).
Skard, T. (1981), 'Progress for Women: Increased Female Representation in Political Elites in Norway', in Epstein, C. and Coser, R. (eds), *Access to Power* (Allen and Unwin).
Skelcher, C. (1983), 'Towards Salaried Councillors? – The Special Responsibility Allowances', *Local Government Studies*, Vol. 19, no. 3 (pp. 10–13).
Stacey, M. and Price, M. (1981), *Women in Power and Politics* (Tavistock).
Stack, H. J. (1970), 'Grass Roots Militants and Ideology', *Polity*, Vol. 2, no. 4 (pp. 426–42).

Stanyer, J. (1977), 'Electors, Candidates and Councillors: Some Technical Problems in the Study of Political Recruitment Processes in Local Government', *Policy and Politics*, Vol. 6 (pp. 71–92).

Stewart, J. and Stoker, G. (eds) (1989), *The Future of Local Government* (Macmillan).

Stoker, G. (1988), *The Politics of Local Government* (Macmillan).

Stoker, G. (1989), 'Creating a Local Government for a Post-Fordist Society: The Thatcherite Project?', in Stewart, J. and Stoker, G. (eds), *The Future of Local Government* (Macmillan).

Thomas Report (1982), *Support Services for Councillors* (Association of Councillors).

The Times Educational Supplement, 29 January 1988.

Travers, T. (1986a), 'An Honourable Draw? Local versus Central Government in the 1970s and 1980s', *Public Money*, December 1986.

Travers, T. (1986b), *The Politics of Local Government Finance* (Allen and Unwin).

Travers, T. (1988), 'Reform is Bad News for Local Autonomy', *Local Government Chronicle* 12 August 1988.

Travers, T. (1989), 'Community Charge and Other Financial Changes', in Stewart, J. and Stoker, G. (eds), *The Future of Local Government* (Macmillan).

Walker, D. (1983), 'Local Interests and Representation: The Case of "Class" Interest among Labour Representatives in Inner London', *Government and Policy*, Vol. 1.

Welch, S. and Studlar, D. (1988), 'The Effects of Candidate Gender on Voting for Local Office in England', *British Journal of Political Science*, Vol. 18, Part 2 (pp. 273–86).

Westwood, S. (1984), *All Day, Every Day* (Pluto Press).

Wheeler, L., Reiss, H., and Nezlak, J. (1983), 'Loneliness, Social Interaction and Sex Roles', *Journal of Personality and Social Psychology*, Vol. 45, no. 4 (pp. 943–53).

Widdicombe (1986a), *The Conduct of Local Authority Business: Report of the Committee of Inquiry into the Conduct of Local Authority Business* (HMSO).

Widdicombe (1986b), *Research Volume I: The Political Organisation of Local Authorities* (HMSO).

Widdicombe (1986c), *Research Volume II: The Local Government Councillor* (HMSO).

Widdicombe (1986d), *Research Volume III: The Local Government Elector* (HMSO).

Widdicombe (1986e), *Research Volume IV: Aspects of Local Democracy* (HMSO).

Willmott, P. and Young, M. (1975), *The Symmetrical Family* (Penguin).

Wimbush, E. and Talbot, M. (1989) (eds), *Relative Freedoms? Women and Leisure* (Open University Press).

Yeandle, S. (1984), *Women's Working Lives* (Tavistock).

Young, K. and Kramer, J. (1978), *Strategy and Conflict in Metropolitan Housing: Suburbia Versus the Greater London Council* (Heinemann).

Young, K. (1985), *Local Government and the Environment* in Jowell, R. and Witherspoon, S. (1985), op. cit.

Young, K. and Mills, L. (1980), *Public Policy Research: A Review of Qualitative Methods* (SSRC Monograph: School Government Publishing Company).

Index